AMERICA
AT THE ABYSS:
WILL AMERICA SURVIVE?

AMERICA
AT THE ABYSS:
WILL AMERICA SURVIVE?

TOM DONELSON

LIBERTY HILL PUBLISHING

Liberty Hill Publishing
2301 Lucien Way #415
Maitland, FL 32751
407.339.4217
www.libertyhillpublishing.com

Paperback ISBN-13: 978-1-6628-3672-5
Hard Cover ISBN-13: 978-1-6628-3673-2
Ebook ISBN-13: 978-1-6628-3674-9

Table of Contents

Opening

During the 2016 primary, I did not support Donald Trump. I viewed him as 17th out of 17th candidates for the Presidency and I was not alone. Many conservatives viewed Trump with suspicion and wondered who was the real Donald Trump? He was a Republican before flirting with running for President through what was left of Perot's Reform Party in 2000 and he was a registered Democrat from 2001 to 2009 before switching back to the Republican party. He was as likely to contribute to Democrats as to Republicans. There was no consistent Trump philosophy other than he was a protectionist on trade issues.

He had four bankruptcies in his business career but landed on his feet before increasing his wealth. Married three times, he was often featured on tabloids and during the 2016 primary, Trump, for his talk about conservative ideas, occasionally turned back to his liberal views throughout the election cycle when he got into trouble or looked for answers when stumped. During the Wisconsin primary, he attacked Scott Walker's reforms from the left when he stated that Walker should have surrendered to the unions and raised taxes. He simply recited leftist talking points in Wisconsin—and this was not the first time in this election that he would resort to leftist talking points. Over the past twenty years before 2016, Trump's views included many leftist ideas: taxing the rich, single-payer health care, gun control, pro-abortion positions.

Trump did not look like a conservative and before he ran, not really a Republican, even though in the eyes of his supporters this was a benefit.

In his presidency, Trump promoted conservative ideas. Many of his ideas were traditional Republican ones, including marginal tax reduction along with tax cuts that benefitted all taxpayers. His war on regulations liberated the economy. His tax plans resembled what Marco Rubio proposed in the 2016 primary and his original proposal for corporate tax rates were similar what Ted Cruz proposed. His immigration reforms were what *National Review* supported and his Supreme Court appointments were as conservative as any appointed by any Republican including Reagan. The fear many of us had about Trump had disappeared by his actions and many of our objections became moot.

Trump did not reduce spending nor was he anxious to reform entitlements, but as we will see further in this book, many of his supporters did not support any major reforms for many want these entitlements. In the past decade, many of these Middle Americans saw their income decline while much of the heartland was being hollowed out. Entitlements will *have* to be reformed eventually. Without bipartisan agreement and the understanding that many Americans need these entitlements, reform will be a political failure.

Trump challenged free trade orthodoxy. While the economic case for free trade is easily made, try to explain to the average Walmart worker the benefit of free trade and he or she will point to an empty building down the road and tell you, "This was a factory where I used to work but now that factory is in China, and I am a greeter at Walmart." Trump's instinct is that of a protectionist but the one trade treaty that he did negotiate, the updating of NAFTA, he did not shut the borders to trade but made adjustments that benefitted his base in Middle America and yet he continued the basic principle of liberalized trade. He threatened Mexico with tariffs and, he worked out a deal to have Mexico help restrict immigration into the United States. The case of tariffs against China dealt with more than just protectionism but also weakening a potential enemy who used trade as a tool to strengthen their own economy while running a corporatist economy that violated their share of trade agreements including theft of intellectual property. We can debate the efficacy of these trade tariffs against China, but the reasons for Chinese tariffs were more than just about trade.

Trump's successes were often overshadowed by his personality. *Claremont Review of Books* editor Charles Kesler observed, "Well, I think he had a chance. His message, his policies, could have been very helpful in carving out a new middle in American politics. The problem was his tone, his affect, his showmanship, and egotism, whatever you want to call it exactly, undercut that political attempt, and it left him in the strange position of governing a country in which 60 percent of the people in one poll said that they were better off now than they were four years before, and yet 20 percent of those people voted against him... So, he turned out a lot of pro-Trump voters, but he also turned out a lot of anti-Trump voters. He threw away whatever chance he had to be a unifying figure. And if you look at some of the micro-results, he did better among some Black voters and Hispanic voters in various places. So, the simple story of Donald Trump the racist can't be entirely true. Despite his personality, or maybe because of his personality, he gave them some hope. That's why I think it might have been a winnable election for Trump, if he had just been a little less Trump-like in his personality."

Thus, the double edge sword that was Trump. As Kesler observed, "But it's also economic dislocations and what has happened to the middle class and to the working class in America. I do not think any of that is irrecoverable, though. And I think we can do better. But I do think that, yeah, in some ways, I fear we are hollowing out the republic. You have two adamant parties that increasingly deplore each other, and which of these parties has the time to take up the banner of the original republic? Which party cares about individual rights, about natural rights, about limited government, about a whole set of constitutional ideas that we were once so proud of, but which figure only at the margins of our constitutional and political arguments?"[1]

The Trump whose tone turned off enough voters, is also the Trump who advanced the conservative cause by defending basic American values, fought against cancel culture, and promoted conservative values and policies. In 2016, I was a reluctant supporter of Trump but in 2020, he was the man standing between radical socialist idea that is now taking root in Washington and the rest of us who will become the victims of this new radicalism.

To this point, Charles Kesler added, "But he did stand up for the traditional, patriotic civic culture. And he was one of the very few Republican politicians who had really any interest in tackling political correctness, or the eventual toppling of monuments and statues, which I think was very defensible on civic or nationalist grounds. This is part of what made Trump so attractive to a lot of voters."[3]

Four years ago, I wrote that the Democratic Party was becoming the party of democratic socialism. The trends I noted have become true. The Democrats are the socialist party of America. Trump has changed the conservative movement and the Republican Party and has given us both a coalition to build upon and a philosophy that can combine his populism with conservative ideals. We are looking at the abyss, but this book is designed to follow up on my previous book and various articles and reports for the Americas Majority Foundation on combining the best of Trump's populism with conservative ideals. I came of age in Reagan's era and for the past four years, I have had a podcast twice a week and had my chance to talk with not just my fellow conservatives but also many on the left. Talking with and debating those on the left and helps us fully understand the threats we face.

We are facing the dangerous threat of a political movement from the left that is abandoning much of what made America great. My goal in this book is to explain what we should do to counter the left and preserve America.

Tom Donelson
March 30th, 2021

The Leadership Class Crisis

America's leadership class is in crisis beginning with our political class which includes the party leadership of both Parties, bureaucrats running the administrative state, the foreign policy experts that populate both think tanks and administrations, depending on which party is in power.

Trump had to depend on many within the establishment as he started his administration. This proved to be one of his Achilles heels, as many of these individuals did not buy into his agenda, including foreign policy where the amateurs proved to be more effective in implementing Trump's goals than the foreign policy experts. This was shown in the Middle East as the Trump foreign policy team produced an anti-Iranian Sunni alliance with Israel in the Middle East. This overcame one of Obama's great foreign policy mistakes, the Iranian nuclear deal. He and his amateurs saw changes in the Middle East that his experts didn't see, such as how states such as the United Arab Emirates could be potential allies of Israel. The amateurs took advantages of those changes and made steps towards peace. Trump saw the threat of China that his experts did not see or refused to see. We will now see if Biden's foreign policy experts can match Trump's foreign policy record in the Biden administration. (I am keeping my finger crossed but not putting much hope in Biden's foreign relations team.)

The scientific class was a major failure in 2020 as this was the year when the pursuit of scientific truth died and may be incapable of being resurrected. The Wuhan virus demonstrated that our scientific class was perfectly willing to fit their science into political conventional wisdom, resulting in hundreds of thousands of deaths and the destruction of the world economy and local communities. Our scientists may have killed more people prematurely than they saved from the virus. The academic class has replaced teaching with indoctrination and the media class is merely an appendage of the political class, and the Democratic Party. As one wise pundit noted, "Media members are Democratic operatives with bylines."

Glenn Harlan Reynolds described the suicide of expertise: "It was the experts — characterized in terms of their self-image by David Halberstam in *The Best and the Brightest* — who brought us the twin debacles of the Vietnam War, which we lost, and the War On Poverty, where we spent trillions and certainly didn't win. In both cases, confident assertions by highly credentialed authorities foundered upon reality, at a dramatic cost in blood and treasure. Mostly other people's blood and treasured, and these are not isolated failures."[2]

Over the past decade, we have seen the Great Recession, due to a housing bubble engineered by existing laws and promoted by the best and brightest on Wall Street. Trump inherited a foreign policy debacle in the Middle East engineered by Obama's experts, who produced a policy that led to hundreds of thousands of deaths, a million refugees headed for Europe, the rise of ISIS, and the upending of previous relations between the U.S. and the State of Israel. Nor can we forget the toppling of Moammar Gadhafi, which led to Libya becoming yet another sanctuary for Islamic terrorists and another places where refugees fled the Middle East for Europe. A year after the toppling of Gadhafi, attack on two United States facilities resulted in the death of Ambassador Christopher Stevens and three others.

Glenn Harlan Reynolds concluded, "If experts want to reclaim a position of authority, they need to make a few changes. First, they should make sure they know what they're talking about, and they shouldn't talk about things where their knowledge isn't solid. Second, they should be appropriately modest in their claims of authority. And third, they should check their egos. It doesn't matter what your SAT scores were, voters are under no obligation to listen to you unless they find what you say persuasive." [3]Modesty is not a trait that this generation of the Leadership class has demonstrated. The elites have done well while the ordinary folks in fly over country have seen their incomes plummet and their ability to make a fortune shrivel. The expert class who guided America from the 1940 to the 1960's won a world war, designed a bipartisan policy of containment that prevented World War III and a victory over the Soviet Empire presided over by two members of that generation, Ronald Reagan and George H.W. Bush. The Greatest Generation discovered vaccines for polio, antibiotics that saved lives, and sent a man to the moon. Jet planes and space flights were dreams that became reality and it was that generation that began to redress the wrongs done to our Black citizens. The present generation of experts may have given us computers, and the computing power in our hands is greater that what took Apollo flights to the Moon. While planes have become faster, the time to get from point A to B is longer and while cars may have advantages over the cars of the 1950's, the average person in 1950 would have little trouble recognizing or driving what we drive today. There are no flying cars and we are replacing reliable nuclear power with less reliable energy derived from wind and solar power. The electric car is a century-old technology that is hardly a major advance in automotive history. And again, where are the flying cars?

In 2016, Many Americans supported Trump because they resented the Leadership class and their insulation from the results of their policy. This century has hardly been a success for the Leadership class. The Leadership class is not a meritocracy and while many in the leadership class worry about the Q Anon conspiracy, the Leadership class believed their own conspiracy theories, like the Russian collusion hoax that had Trump being a puppet of Putin. (Considering that Trump policies were even tougher on Putin than previous administrations, Putin didn't get his money worth from his supposed puppet.)

America finally left Afghanistan featuring a disastrous withdrawal engineered by Biden administration. At the end of Afghanistan, we had soldiers who weren't even born when 9/11 occurred, and many Middle-Class jobs disappeared at home. Richard Fernandez tweeted, "The elites lost their mojo by becoming absurd. It happened on the road between cultural appropriation and transgender bathrooms…People believe from instinct. The Roman gods became ridiculous when the Roman emperors did. PC is the equivalent of Caligula's horse." [4]

While many in the Middle Class saw their income and wealth decline, they were often mocked when they rebelled by voting for Trump and that includes a few within the conservative ranks, some of whom didn't even vote for him either in 2016 or 2020 and supported the two impeachment attempts.

The election of Joe Biden and Kamala Harris in 2020 shows the complete failure of the Leadership class. Biden was a mediocrity at his best but the one thing he was good at, he knew how to play the system and enrich his family and himself. Nor was this the usual graft as his family profited as his son made billions in deals with China while Biden as vice president was negotiating deals that cost many Middle Americans their jobs and allowed China to become even more powerful. Biden also got a prosecutor in Ukraine fired for investigating a corrupt company that Hunter Biden was making hundreds of thousands a year from. (Let us not forget that Trump was impeached over raising the issue of Hunter Biden with Ukrainian president Volodymyr Zelensky. Trump got impeached over asking about what a corrupt Presidential candidate did when he was the Vice President in a previous administration.)

Richard Fernandez noted in 2017, "Suicidal factionalism has torn apart famous nations before, Rome's Crisis of the Third Century being the most famous example. . .. If Trump is overthrown by the Deep State in a year, he's unlikely to be the last. If neither faction will suffer itself to be governed by the other, whoever succeeds Trump can expect his term to be short. America could have its own period of the <u>26 presidents</u>. That will be good news for the Barbarians, waiting at the edge of the Baltics, in the South China Sea, and on Europe's borders, ready to move in. Rome's Third Century crisis did not end well. The new normal was not a return to the Golden Age, but the end of it."[5] In 2020, the Leadership class won this battle and essentially turned the country over to the socialists and oligarchies that fund their political activity.

Glenn Harlan Reynolds noted, "Strong nations can fail when their leadership class, or a part of it, succumbs to pettiness, and places its narrow factional interests above those of the nation. Americans have often assumed that we are immune to such things. *Perhaps earlier Americas, with a more disciplined, more patriotic ruling class, were. But today's America is not. Beware.*"[6]

Right now, the conservative movement is in turmoil, not exactly sure what to do in the wake of the 2020 elections. The second impeachment of Trump only added more wounds to conservatives and risks further factionalism of the movement, as did the January 6th riots in Washington. The Trump presidency is controversial among conservatives. since he was not a typical conservative of the past five decades. For those of us who came of age in the Reagan years, Trump challenged our ideas. However, times and circumstances change, and we need to recognize that while conservative principles are still essential, the solutions we have come up with to public policy problems need to be reviewed.

Over the past four years, our coalition is shifting, beginning with adding blue-collar workers living in medium size cities. rural areas and small towns, and we are adding minorities who are finding that states run by Democrats don't work and give them with fewer job opportunities and higher crime than they would in red states. We have developed losses with suburbanites, but we don't know whether these losses were due to the temperament of Trump that they didn't like or something deeper.

The other shift is that the business class has changed, with many of the larger business leaders siding with the left in the culture war and becoming more caretakers than innovators. Even the tech companies that drove much of the economic growth in the 1980's and 1990's have ceased to be innovators. but instead have become monopolies but monopolies that are willing to perform censorship demanded by the political class, who want to crush any opponents who dare to resist the coming socialism of America. These monopolies want to use government to set up regulations to destroy their competitors.

When Apple, Facebook and Twitter went after Parler, they had two objectives: to crush a conservative competitor and to censor conservative thoughts. The past two election cycles 2018 and 2020, Republicans have been outspent by Democrats and much of this due to big business and big tech money going to the Democrats.

In my last book and reports for Americas Majority Foundation, I have made the case for the synergy between Trump populism and conservatism, and I've warned if we failed to form an alliance, then many of our coalition will either stay home or move to the left. Conservatism is at stake but there are solutions to preserving conservative principles beginning with studying the past.

William McKinley in 1896, like Ronald Reagan in 1980, attracted a coalition that lasted a third of a century. While the Trump coalition has yet to be solidified, the Reagan coalition lasted thru the 2004 elections and enough of the coalition remained, aided by additional blue-collar workers gave Trump the edge in 2016 and most of them stayed with Trump and the GOP in 2020. Trump is building on a changing Republican coalition and much of the old Reagan coalition has been fraying, with parts of it lost to the left.

McKinley put his own Trumpian coalition that lasted until 1932 before Herbert Hoover, a moderate Republican, turned a recession into the Great Depression. McKinley is viewed as a big business Republican but there is more to the story as McKinley put a winning coalition in 1896 and cemented it in 1900. Among his clients as a lawyer was representing coal miners after a violent strike. He took the case pro bono and got all but one worker acquitted, and his presidential run included many of these workers. The Republicans were born in 1856 as a party opposing slavery but after the Civil War, Republicans found themselves seeking causes to unite voters behind after Reconstruction. Protectionism through tariffs became that issue but during the 1890's, monetary policy became the new issue as the debate over the gold standard and the roles of big business and monopolies in the American economy dominated politics.

In 1896, McKinley ran on a platform of sound money and using tariffs to protect American industries, promoting higher wages and prosperity. The majority of America agreed with the Republican platform and in 1900, victory in the Spanish-American War and four years of prosperity led to an even larger Republican victory. McKinley proved to be a good manager of the country, taking advantages of events as they unfolded and combining them into a coherent policy. His style was not flashy like his vice-president and successor Theodore Roosevelt, who built upon the policies and ideas McKinley created. McKinley's manners as president gave comfort to a nation during an era when America became less rural and more urban and became a world power.

We are in midst of a significant transition of America in this decade. The conservative movement is being challenged as America changes, much as they were in the 1970's and 1890's of a changing America and adopting ideas to fit those needs. In the 1890's, Republicans used tariffs to protect American business, but the McKinley era saw higher wages for workers and these policies continued to work for many including the working and middle classes in the early 20th century. Many free traders would find objections to these policies, but McKinley was dealing with another time, and he lived in an America *where there was no extensive welfare state or Federal involvement in our economy* and was just becoming a world power as result of the Spanish American War. Government spending was significantly lower than today. McKinley adopted policies that fit his era and built a coalition and the minimal government activism allowed for America to become a world power both militarily and economically.

Reagan lived in an era in which inflation pushed many in the middle class were pushed into high marginal tax rates once reserved for the upper class. A stagnating economy combined with double-digit inflation to produce "stagflation." In addition, Reagan had to confront an expanding Soviet Empire.at the end of the 1970's. Many observers in this period saw America in permanent decline. Reagan's tax rate reductions and victory in the Cold War and winning the cold war produced world peace and nearly a quarter century of prosperity. Most Americans saw their income rise and by 2007, 63% of Americans became investors.

Trump inherited a foreign policy mess. Yemen, stable before Obama took office, was in a civil war with proxy forces of Iran and Saudi Arabia, Ukraine was under siege and partially occupied by Putin's forces. ISIS occupied much of Syria and Iraq and Chinese influence steadily grew. The economy was growing slowly, with *many Americans were not sharing into the growth.* Many in the middle class found their overall wealth declining as their wages stagnated.

Trump had foreign-policy successes, including formation of an anti-Iranian coalition including Arab states and Israel. Many Americans did see their income go up until the pandemic, which helped sink his chances for a second term. Many of his policies were center-right and his foreign policy represented a chance to restructure our overseas priorities. We will see if this can be resurrected in 2024 if Biden returns to the foreign policy failures of the Obama/Biden Administration.

The greater threat to our freedom comes from the democratic socialist movement. While a reform conservative movement can embrace rising national populism, there are no counterpoints on the right to the democratic socialist movement, since many moderates have either been defeated in elections or have simply left the Democratic Party. The Democratic donor class funds the socialist movement with glee, and the Democratic Party has become the party of the very rich and the poor. As the Democratic Party has shown since Obama's presidency, they have no problem in using government to attack their opponents including the use of the IRS to target conservative political organizations. The left likes to portray Trump as the second coming of Hitler or Mussolini, but it has been the Democratic Party which is a real threat to many of our freedoms, beginning with free speech and free political association.

I observed that during the 2016 election, the future of conservative ideas was being fought between Marco Rubio and Ted

Cruz. Rubio and Cruz's families both came to America from Cuba, but even though they were both Cuban-Americans, but this hid the differences between the two and the emerging Hispanic community. Rubio, like most Hispanics, is Roman Catholic, but Cruz is Southern Baptist; and a rising number of Hispanics are evangelicals. Before Rubio was elected to the Senate, he was a Florida legislator including being the speaker of the Florida House. Cruz worked in George W. Bush's Department of Justice and the Federal Trade Commission before becoming the solicitor general of Texas, where he argued cases in front of the Supreme Court. Cruz drafted the amicus brief for *Heller*, a significant victory for gun rights in 2008 supported by 31 state attorney generals.

The differences between the two reflected the differences within the Republican Party. Rubio's tax plan depended on tax credits for the middle class. His goal was to promote family values and help the middle class through tax reform. Rubio's plan left the top rate at 35%, which is only a slight drop from the present system and. Of all the tax reform proposals between 2010 and 2016, Rubio's plan had the highest marginal tax rates. Ted Cruz proposed a flat 10 percent tax plus a 16 percent rate on business transactions that was like a value added tax. In foreign affairs, Rubio campaigned as more of an interventionist whereas Cruz's foreign policy was a return to the pre-9/11 more modest view of America's role in the world.

Trump's individual tax plans were similar to Rubio's and his business plan was similar to what Cruz proposed. Trump's foreign policy was a return to a more modest view of foreign affairs based on defending American interests and not being involved in parts of the world that may be part of America's interests.

Both Cruz and Rubio are social conservatives and supporters of gun rights but that is the norm for Republicans even in the era of Trump. Cruz argued Second Amendment cases in front of the Supreme Court and Cruz opposed crony capitalism including ethanol and sugar subsidies. (Rubio supported sugar subsidies because Florida politicians support sugar subsidies just as Iowa politicians support ethanol.) As the Carrier case in Indiana demonstrated after the 2016 election, in which Trump used government power to aid the company, Trump supported his version of crony capitalism if it benefited his voters.

Both Cruz and Rubio are considered potential rivals for 2024, but the field has expanded to include South Dakota governor Kristi Noem, former South Carolina governor Nikki Haley and Florida governor Ron DeSantis. During the pandemic, Governor Noem and Governor DeSantis showed leadership at keeping economic growth in their respective states while dealing with a pandemic and showed that much of the scientific class advice coming from Washington *was not just wrong, but disastrous to many Middle-Class Americans, small businesses, and city residents, while failing to save lives.* Noem and DeSantis ignored much of the Scientific class's advice emanating from Washington. They instead listened to the "skeptics" whose ideas and solutions proven more correct. (I only use the word 'skeptics' because many of those who opposed lockdown strategies proved to be more accurate with their science, but the Media class and much of the political class viewed them as outliers as opposed to scientists who "got the virus right".)

Underneath the disappointment of 2020 included Trump's challenges of the election and the January 6th riot in which a group of right-wingers attacked the Capitol. These actions left many conservatives in a depressed mood and wondering what to do next. Many were ready to be rid of Trump and others were ready for Trump's second chapter. The real need is for the conservative leadership to accept the fact that Trump's supporters are here to stay and are a necessary part of the coalition without which Republican and conservatives can't win. As for Trump, he will remain a Republican to ensure that his ideas are still part of the debate and his supporters respected. The one obstacle to Trump's future is that Biden Department of Justice will continue to persecute Trump and his family and there will be attacks from Democratic state attorney generals as well. Trump may suffer the fate of Andrew Mellon, the secretary of Treasury in the Harding, Coolidge, and Hoover administration. Mellon spent his last years fighting off Democrats' efforts to put him in jail for various tax crimes. Shortly after his death, Mellon would be exonerated. Democrats want not just to defeat Trump but also to humiliate him and his family, hoping to permanently blacken Trump's legacy.

The good news is that Republicans have a deep bench for 2024 among both governors and legislators in Washington, but too many within the Republican establishment are just as happy not just to see Trump leave but his supporters as well. Without these Trump voters, there is no chance of a Republican victory. As I noticed in my previous book, many of Trump's domestic policy ideas are in line with much of modern-day Republican and conservative principles and his foreign policy are becoming more in line with Americans wary of war and endless American military deployments. The potential to synergize conservative ideas with Trump populism is there, but it means that the conservative leadership class must change course and stop resisting Trump's supporter and instead take advantage where his ideas mesh with conservative ideas.

My book *The Rise of National Populism and Democratic Socialism: What Our response Should Be*, explored how, if 2020 showed anything, we are a 50/50 nation, but the left holds the advantage as they control the leadership class, including the media class, much of the political class, the scientific class, and the academic class. We are witnessing the implosion of these classes, *but their decline is also leading to the decline of America.* The political class is the leading governing class that encompasses much of

Washington including the administrative state, congressional legislators, the Democratic Party and even quite a few leaders of the
Republican Party. The governing class extends to many governors
like Andrew Cuomo who proved disastrous in running his state,
implementing policies that resulted in the death of many senior
citizens and trashing his state economy. (He was forced from office
due to sexual assault and harassment of women but not for a policy
resulting in the deaths of thousands of senior citizens.)

As Joel Kotkin noted, *"One has to go back to Reagan to find a
Republican Party that could consistently position itself as populist.
Reagan's appeal was based on security and taxes; for today's GOP,
the issue should be – besides terrorism and rising crime – how to
address the decline of the middle- and working-class economy".*[7] In
the past, Democrats appealed to the middle class with programs
designed for them, such as the G.I. Bill and had no problem with
fighting class warfare. Hillary Clinton's campaign attempted to
appeal to the middle class through welfare expansion geared
strictly to middle class voters but Hillary Clinton, like Obama,
built a Democratic base based less than on class and more on race
and identity politics and Biden is continuing this trend. Many of
this new left-wing coalition is built around Millennials, minorities,
single people, academics, and wealthy tech executives. Obama's
rejection of the Keystone XL pipeline and his war on fossil fuels
was a dagger aimed at many blue-collar Democrats, including
union members. With coal mines closing due to EPA regulations,
many blue-collar voters who voted for Bill Clinton in 1992 were
abandoned by his wife and her party in 2016. Biden is abandoning
these voters as he seeks to increase Democratic suburban voters
while maintaining minority voters. His opening executive orders
blocking the Keystone XL Pipeline and energy development on
federal land has affected blue states like New Mexico and Colorado,
who are now seeing their energy sector trashed. Many blue voters

are now seeing the price of voting Democratic. As H.L. Mencken noted, "Democracy is the theory that the common people know what they want and deserve to get it good and hard." These voters got it hard, and this is only the beginning.

For four decades, the Republicans have depended upon a coalition of social conservatives, national security hawks and supply siders. But this coalition that elected Reagan is now fraying and is no longer the majority. The good news is that the left has abandoned blue-collar white voters as well as many within their minority base who have more in common with these white, blue-collar voters than with other parts of the Democratic base. These minorities own their businesses and are moving into the middle class, but they are seeing doors to opportunity being shut by the oligarchies that fund the Democratic left. At least more 1.5 million Blacks and Hispanics voted for Trump in 2020 than in 2016. The door is open for Republicans and reformist conservatives who understand that the Republican Party is now the party of Main Street. It is time for Wall Street to understand their long-term health is dependent upon a healthy Main Street. Wall Street can't survive in the long run if nothing is produced on Main Street.

The Republicans will have the opportunity to rebuild a new conservative majority, based on conservative ideals beginning with this: *the average American wants and needs a Fair Opportunity to Succeed.* The challenge to the conservative leadership is to complement conservative ideals with the populist aspect of the movement to form a more permanent coalition. The present leadership class is no longer adequate to govern America and changes are coming, and we conservatives need to be the vanguard of those changes.

I wrote in 2017, "Trump has many failings including making a fortune as a crony capitalist making his own deals with government regulators and Democratic politicians, but part of his appeal lies with his own view of the political class which he is forever calling 'stupid.' He understands that much of America no longer trusts government, but this distrust goes to other institutions of the ruling class, including corporations and Wall Street. Trump appeals to independents and working-class Democrats who know the old rules of the game no longer work for them, ensuring and they are alienated from politics."[8]

On January 28th, a group of amateurs took on Melvin Capital as Melvin Capital decided to short GameStop, a struggling company, gambling that GameStop was about done as a corporation. A group r/wallstreetbets on Reddit acted and bought shares in GameStop to raise GameStop prices, thwarting Capital efforts to short the stock and costing hedge funds billions. This was a battle of David and Goliath, with David using his slingshot to knock down Goliath, and then decapitating billions from the giant hedge fund. Glenn Reynolds wrote, "Joe Biden is president. Democrats control the House and Senate. Tech overlords are quashing dissent. We're in the middle of what our betters call the "Great Reset," when the power of big institutions and the Really Smart People™ is supposed to be re-established after the unfortunate deviation of the Trump years. The *hoi polloi* is supposed to know their place now, especially those annoying loudmouths on the Internet… This position came to attention of the r/wallstreetbets group on Reddit, and some of its members decided to give Melvin a hotfoot. Members of the group, who often invest via the youth-oriented platform Robinhood Markets, started buying shares in GameStop… This display of spontaneous group power by a bunch of previously unknown investors has frightened the Really Smart People™ and led to reactions that will make things worse, not better. Some discount brokers started displaying warnings and limiting trades. Discord, a popular online chat service used by the r/wallstreetbets group, shut down the group's service, offering them no alternative …The Robinhood Markets investors are neither truly left nor right as we defined them in the past, but it is about Suicide of Expertise we will be allowed go up or be forced to stay down. Regulators huffed and puffed as CNBC had industry big shots yelling that they the little guys shouldn't "be allowed be allowed to do this...Reddit mob was just doing to the short-sellers what Wall Street insiders do all the time to retail investors."

This incident showed early in the Biden Administration that populism was not just Trumpian but included people right to left. The leadership class and much of the business class are no longer respected, much less liked by the masses. Glenn H. Reynolds noted, "The Big Guys' problem is that nobody likes them much. From Silicon Valley to Wall Street, they're deeply unpopular with ordinary Americans, on both the left and the right, resentment they've stoked with selfishness, arrogance and condescension. Their solution to this unpopularity has been to use their control over online platforms, and their influence over the government, to silence their critics."[9]

What Trump did was to expose the Leadership class for what they have become, people willing to do anything to keep power. Trump showed how much removed the Leadership class is from the American public and he left in place a coalition that can be expanded and take power back from the Leadership class in 2024.

Economic Policies: Where Do We Go?

Throughout 2020, we at the Americas Majority Foundation reviewed data comparing Republican-run states and Democratic-run states as well states with hard lockdowns and non-lockdown states. Every week we kept tabs on the percentage of unemployment of the working population, in a state, death from COVID-19 per capita, and total deaths from COVID-19.

In addition, Wilfred Reilly, a political scientist at Kentucky State, did two studies for Americas Majority Foundation on the impact of the lockdowns, both on number of cases and deaths along with impact on unemployment. Professor Reilly conducted a study in April 2020 that questioned the effectiveness of the lockdown and in his two studies for us, he followed up to see the impact of the lockdown four months later and added comparisons between red states and blue states, including seeing how Blacks and Hispanics fared in the states.

As 2020 closed out, the average unemployment of red states was 5 percent and 2.7 percent of the working population of those states claimed unemployment, while the unemployment rate in blue states was 6.8 percent. with 4 percent of the civilian working population collecting unemployment claims. (The unemployment numbers were for December 2020 and unemployment claims were based on January numbers)

Unemployment and percentage of workers receiving unemployment claims

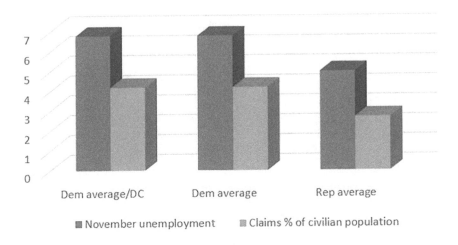

■ November unemployment   ▨ Claims % of civilian population

Our recent weekly data around the time of Biden's inauguration saw that nearly 238,000 died of COVID-19 in blue states for an average of 10,500 deaths per million residents vs. 197,000 deaths and an average of nearly 7300 deaths per million residents in red states.

total death red vs blue states

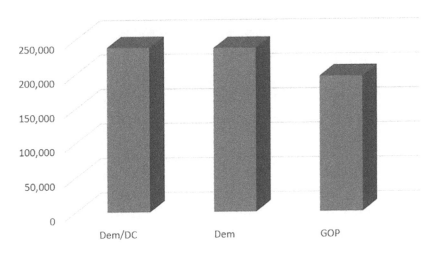

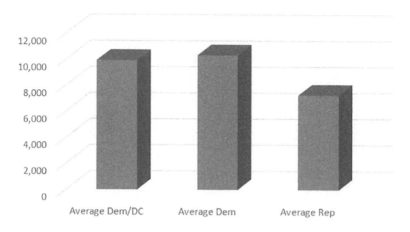

Blue states averaged over 1350 deaths per million residents while red states averaged 1247 deaths per million residents, so there was not real significant difference between the two. Throughout the pandemic in 2020, Democratic' governors on the average restricted economic restrictions more often as an effort to reduce the infections, but these restrictions failed to stem death to COVID-19 compared to red states that did not implement lockdowns and their unemployment rates showed that blue states saw higher unemployment, and failed at protecting their citizens from the virus. Many paid a heavy price for the lockdown through businesses forced to close and jobs lost without any effect on lives saved.

From Thanksgiving thru Biden's inauguration, nearly 90,000 per million residents in blue states died from COVID-19 versus nearly 80,000 per million residents in red states.

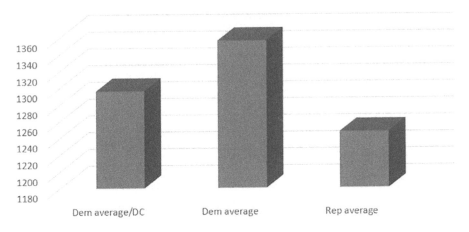

death per capita

Nationally, unemployment dropped from 14.7 percent in April to 6.7 percent in December 2020. In 1957, the flu pandemic killed 100,000 to 115,000 and this would be on a per capita basis today between 160, 000 to 230,000. The 1950's were a decade of high tax rates with the highest at 90 percent and there were three recessions from 1949 to 1960. The Federal Reserve tightened monetary policy in 1957, but the pandemic certainly had impact on the rising unemployment rates at the time. It is hard to detect what impact the pandemic had on in causing the recession of 1957 and what impact government policies had. Trying to figure out what caused the economic downturn is not so simple but a pandemic that killed the equivalent of 200,000 today certainly had an economic impact. The last quarter of 1957 saw a drop of minus 4 percent GDP and minus 10 percent GDP in the first quarter of 1958. In spring of 1957, unemployment was 3.7 percent before hitting 5.2% at the end of the year and peaking at 7.5% in July 1958, dropping back to 6.2% in December 1958. In the third and fourth quarters of 1958 the GDP surged back to 10% growth and the GDP's overall decline was less than 1% between 1957-58 so there was a strong recovery that could be classified as a V-shape recovery in the second half of 1958. The recession of 2020 was self-induced beginning in March, as government locked down the economy to reduce pressure on hospitals.

1957-1958 Recession

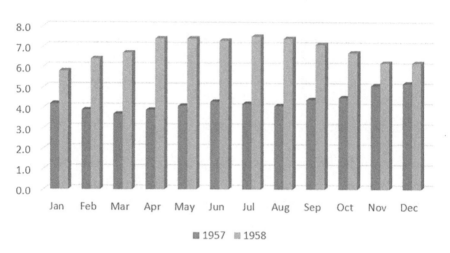

■ 1957 ■ 1958

The 2020 lockdown was supposed to be short term to keep hospitals from overflowing but ended up evolving into economic restrictions that have lasted into 2021. The national unemployment rate was 4.4 percent in March 2020 moving quickly to 14.4 percent in April before dropping to 6.7 percent in December. Economic restrictions by many blue states have artificially kept up the unemployment even higher that would have happened without the restrictions. If Blue states had economic recovery comparable matched that of red states, we would be at about a national 5 percent unemployment rate at the end of 2020 and unemployment continuing into 2021. Nearly half a million of individuals in the restaurants and hospitality business lost their jobs due to economic restrictions re imposed by Democratic governors after Thanksgiving and thru Christmas. This demonstrated that many within the lower and middle classes suffered from the lockdown.

Recovery from depths

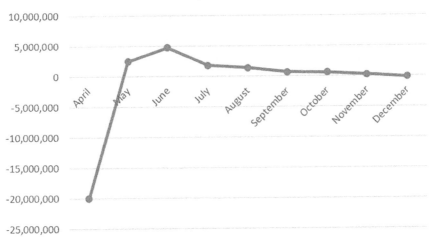

The 1957 and 2020 recessions were fought with different approaches. In the 1957 pandemic, there was no lockdown or any severe economic restrictions. The unemployment rate in that recession only went up to 7.5 percent at its peak. What if we didn't lockdown or simply kept the lockdown at the original timeline of fifteen days before opening and moved to toward a more limited plan that isolated the most vulnerable while allowing younger workers to get back to work? We saw unemployment in 2020 going from a peak of 14.4 percent in April to 6.7 percent in December with an average of 1,500,000 jobs per month returning to the economy from the month of May to the end of the year, representing 60 percent of the jobs recovered from the initial losses. December saw a drop in employment numbers, much of this due to many Democratic governors, including Governor Gavin Newsom of California and Andrew Cuomo of New York, restricting their state's economies. As a result of these restrictions, nearly 500,000 jobs were lost in the restaurant and bar businesses nationwide in 2020. To put the job growth over the last seven-month of 2020, Trump's and red state governors like Ron DeSantis of Florida and Kristi Noem in South Dakota got the unemployment rate in their states below 7% in six months whereas the Obama/Biden administration took five years to get unemployment under 7% in the Great Recession of 2008-09. Unemployment continued to drop to 6 percent in March as the Trump job recovery continued into the Biden administration.

Examining states, we found that top ten states with the lowest unemployment averaged 3.6 percent and the top 25 states averaged 4.4 percent. The 34 states at or under the national average of 6.7 in December averaged 4.9 percent unemployment. Nine of the top 10 states with the lowest unemployment had Republican governors and 17 of the top 25 states had Republican governors. Seventeen of the bottom 25 states had Democratic governors and averaged unemployment rates of 7.4%. Seven of the ten states with the highest unemployment had Democratic governors with an average unemployment in those states of 8.3 percent.

In this study, we compare states with Republican governors with States with Democratic governors. Massachusetts and Maryland were listed as Republican states since they had Republican governors and states like Louisiana, Kansas, and Montana throughout 2020 had Democratic governors were counted as Democratic states. We also reviewed other methodology which we explain further in this chapter. Another methodology compared Republican states in which you have Republican control of legislature and governor seats with Democrat complete control all levers of government as well as those states with both parties sharing power with one party controlling all or some of the legislatures and the other party the governor seat. The results were the same, Republican states had significant less unemployment.

Among the ten states with the highest unemployment include some of the most populous states including New Jersey, Massachusetts, New York, Illinois, Pennsylvania, and California.

This has caused the national unemployment rate to rise as these states make up a third of the United States population. The economic restrictions that remain in force in those large states ensures the national unemployment rate is higher than it should be.

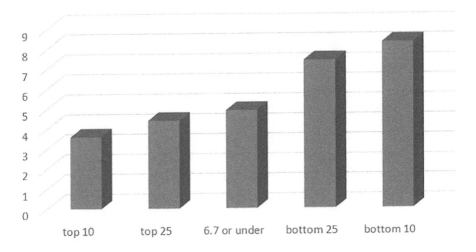

December unemployment 2020

Wilfred Reilly studied the impact of lockdown on unemployment. He compared Democratic states to Republican states as well those states who went for the lockdown compared to non-lockdown states. He found that Republican states had lower unemployment rates. Unemployment in Republican states dropped from 13.2 to 6.5 percent between April and August 2020 and while the rate in Democratic states fell from 15.2 percent to 8.2 percent in the same period. Lockdown states in April saw unemployment rates at 15 percent before dropping to 8.2 percent. Non-lockdown states began with unemployment rates of 10.9 percent before dropping to 5.5 percent[10]

Unemployment red vs blue state, lockdown vs non-lockdown

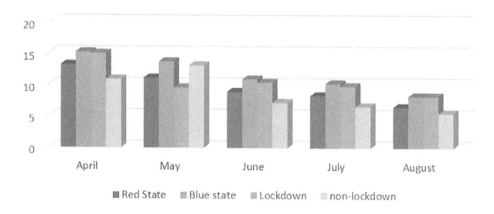

Another example of the devastation of this economic downturn was bankruptcies. In Republicans run states, there were an average of 190 bankruptcies per state per million residents? compared to 246 per million in Democratic states, as well as 256 bankruptcies per million residents in lockdown states and 62 bankruptcies per million residents in non-lockdown states. On a per capita basis, Republican states averaged 33.1 bankruptcies per million residents compared to 34.4 per million in Democratic states, so there wasn't a significant difference on a per capita between Republican and Democratic states, *but there was a significant difference between lockdown and non-lockdown states as lockdown states had 34.4 per million bankruptcies per million residents as opposed to non-lockdown states which had 24.9 bankruptcies per million residents.* Our data shows that the economic devastation caused by the lockdown to local economies as the result of the lockdowns.

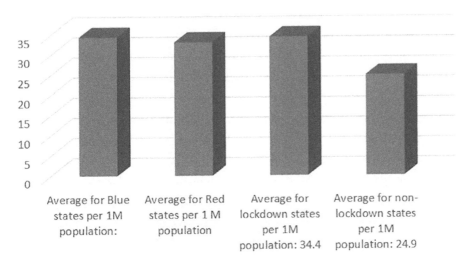

Bankruptcy per million

The original models in March 2020 projected 2,000,000 Americans from COVID-19, numbers comparable to the Spanish flu of 1918-1920 on a per capita basis. We ended up with infectious fatality rates closer to the 1957 and 1968 pandemics, which were more lethal than flu season of the past decade but one tenth as lethal as the 1918-1920 pandemic. The economic lockdown has its own impact, and we will end up more death due to the lockdown than to the virus itself.

Just the News did an analysis on red versus blue states and found similar results to ours. They compared purple states, red states, and blue states. (They identified blue states as having voted Democratic in the last four presidential elections, and red states as those voted for Republican presidents in the last four elections. Purple states were states that split their votes.) Again, Red States proved superior in economic performances in the Just The News analysis, with average unemployment rates of 6.6 percent while blue states had a average of 10.5 percent unemployment rates. Purple states were in the middle with 7.8 percent unemployment rates but purple states with Republican governors outperformed purple states with Democratic governors, with 7.3 percent unemployment in the Republican purple states vs. 8.2 percent in the Democratic purple states.[11]

Dam McLaughlin, writing for National Review Online, found similar patterns in unemployment rates looking at Bureau of Labor Statistics data for March 2021. He found that eleven states and the District of Columbia had unemployment rates of seven percent or higher, or one point higher than the national unemployment rate of six percent. None of the states had Republican governors, and only two (Louisiana and Pennsylvania) had Republican—controlled legislatures. Twenty states had unemployment rates of 4.7 percent or less. In sixteen of these states, Republicans control the governor-ship and the legislature. Vermont has a Republican governor, Kansas and Wisconsin had Republican legislatures, and Minnesota has a Republican-controlled Senate. The only Democratic-controlled state with a below-average unemployment rate was Maine.

"The *average* Republican-controlled state has a 4.5% unem-ployment rate, more than a point below the national average," McLaughlin writes, while the *average* Democrat-controlled state (including D.C.) has an unemployment rate of 7.2 percent, or more than a point above the national average."[12]

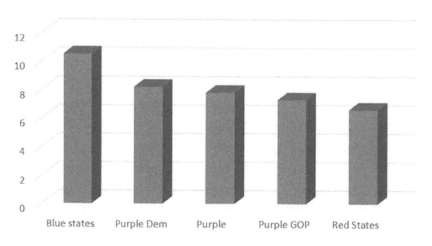

The cost to our society due to lockdown has been high, with increased suicides and delayed treatment for many procedures. A British study showed three million people have forgone cancer screening and 350,000 have delayed cancer treatment. in the UK. In an interview, Martin Kulldorff an epidemiologist at Harvard Medical School, noted, "The media suggests there is a scientific consensus in favor of lockdown, but that is not the case. I have two concerns. *One is about the collateral damage lockdown causes to other aspects of public health.* One of the basic principles of public health is that you do not just look at one disease – you have to look at health as a whole, including all kinds of diseases, over a long period. That is not what has been done with Covid-19. As a public-health scientist, it is stunning to see how focused people are on this one disease and on the short term. The collateral damage is very tragic: cardiovascular disease outcomes are worse, cancer screenings are down, and there are mental-health issues, for example...My second concern is that, even when we put broader public health to one side and focus just on COVID-19, the current approach does not make sense. We sought to flatten the curve in the spring so as not to overload hospitals, and that succeeded in almost every country. *But trying to suppress the disease with contact tracing, testing and isolation, together with severe lockdowns, is not going to solve the problem. It will just push things into the future.*" [13]

Kulldorff points out that the lockdowns proved worse than living with the virus, a virus about as lethal as the 1957 and 1968 flu pandemics. Models released early in the pandemic showed death rates three to five times than what happened, but the scientific class continued to mandate mask wearing, lockdowns, and other economic restrictions in both Europe and the United States.

Our own research conducted by Kentucky State political scientist Wilfred Reilly has shown not only that lockdown did not reduce death from the COVID-19 virus, *but also lockdown states saw an increase of deaths among the general population including blacks and Hispanics* compared to non-lockdown states. [14]A second study by Reilly saw significant decrease of unemployment among non-lockdown states s showed that red states outperformed blue states when it comes to unemployment rates.[15]. This data has been reinforced by our own data that we have collected weekly as well as data collected by Just The News that during the pandemic red states outperformed blue states economically.

A May 2021 National Bureau of Economic Research paper by a research team led by Bentley University economist Dhaval M. Dave complemented our findings. Dave and his associates looked at Texas, the state which was the first to end the lockdown and mask mandates in March 2021. Dave's team found that not only did Covid-19 deaths not rise because of the lockdown, but they *fell* slightly as vaccination rates rose. The fall in Covid cases occurred both in counties in Texas that Donald Trump carried in the 2020 presidential election and those carried by Joseph Biden. However, the end of the lockdown in Texas did not result in a fall in unemployment rates, probably because the additional $300 a week in federal unemployment payments was high enough to discourage recipients from re-entering the labor force.[16]

The highest unemployment rate during the 1957 pandemic was 7.5 percent and by the end of 1957 it was 6 percent. I believe that the national unemployment rate should have been closer to 5 percent or lower at the end of the year. Non-lockdown states averaged 5.5 percent unemployment in August 2020. Without the widespread lockdowns and other severe economic restrictions, our employment rates would be higher and adverse events such as delayed treatment for diseases, increased suicides and higher drug abuse would be reduced. The cost of lockdown due to lost employment, increased bankruptcies and increased deaths will exceed the deaths caused by the virus itself. If the average American were told early in the pandemic that the cost of "flattening the curve" would be higher deaths, record rates, and, hundreds of thousands of small businesses shut down permanently for a virus that may kill no more than two or three people out of 1000, slightly higher than the one out of 1000 death rate annually caused by the flu for the past decade, would they have agreed to these shutdowns?

No academic or scientific advisor has yet to pay a price for the spectacularly gloomy forecasts that guided public policy during the first part of the pandemic. Bad science leads to bad policies, which devastated much of the developed world and put millions in the third world near starvation. Higher poverty, destitution, loss businesses and greater inequality are the price we have paid for this. The one lesson is to become skeptical of our scientific class and understand as we have seen, much of our leading scientific class have been wrong and the skeptics have proven been right. Over 14 000 medical and public heath scientists along with 43,000 medical practitioners have endorsed the Great Barrington Declaration, which calls for Covid-19 fighting policies similar to those enacted by many red state governors such as Kristi Noem in South Dakota and Ron DeSantis in Florida. The declaration calls for strong protections for vulnerable senior citizens in nursing homes but opening the rest of society as much as possible. Lockdowns, the declaration states, lead to "lower childhood vaccination rates, worsening cardiovascular disease outcomes—leading to greater excess mortality in years to come…Keeping students out of school is a grave injustice."[17]

Most Americans don't know that tens of thousands of medical professionals in the U.S. and the world favor a different path from Dr. Fauci and other experts regularly booked on network talk shows who strenuously argue for continued lockdowns, since much of our media has restricted their coverage in favor of pro-lockdown scientists whose forecasts have been proven wrong.

Our research concludes that lockdowns were a failure when continued beyond their original time frame in March and April of 2020. The economic cost of the lockdowns exceeded the benefit of the lockdown's ability to control the spread of the virus. The lockdown did not reduce the number of COVID-19 deaths or cases and the continuous economic restrictions has interfered with our basic liberties and increased economic hardship. The real miracle was that our economy from May 2020 through the end of the year has grown in spite of government policies designed to restrict economic growth.

The economic turndown and slow recovery are the fault of government policies, not free markets. Government told businesses to shut down to stop the pandemic and, as one meme goes, "We had our free trial of socialism, how did you like it?" Yes, it was socialism and many governors and mayors have shown their inner dictator as they issued all kinds of rules and regulations, some of which contradicted each other while destroying economic development and raising unemployment levels to depression levels. The idea of government determining what is "essential" and "non-essential" business is more power than any government should have. Many states opened up earlier than others, so we witnessed a nation rolling in bits and pieces as some states move forward in opening up their economies and other states move forward at a snails' pace, later reversing the progress they made. *As we have seen those states that opened their economies, mostly red states, had lower unemployment and less deaths throughout 2020.*

University of Chicago economist Casey B. Mulligan estimated "that the shutdown of nonessential businesses reduces market production by almost $6 trillion per year of shutdown. Relief efforts further reduce the current value of future economic activity by about $2 trillion per year of shutdown. Black markets and additional time in the nonmarket sector replace about $2 trillion of the $8 trillion of lost market production. I estimate that the value of nonmarket production falls below what it would be if the normal market inputs were available by about $1 trillion per year of shutdown. The sum of these puts the welfare costs at about $7 trillion per year of shutdown." [18]He added that we are looking at either budget cuts or raising taxes nearly 2 trillion dollars to deal with the aftermath of this crisis.

The key to recovery begins with medical innovation that Operation Warp Speed was designed to do, bring those medical discoveries (including new forms of vaccines) that speeded an end to the pandemic. Mulligan estimates that a Covid-19 vaccine would not only save lives but also save 28 billion dollars for each working day once normal activity returns. The key in this pandemic is that the old ways of approving vaccines needed to change, and the Trump administration succeeded with Operation Warp Speed to do exactly that by bringing vaccines from creation to approval within 11 months, instead of the years required for earlier vaccines. As *Washington Post* columnist Megan McArdle observes, the technology that enabled the production of the Pfizer/BioNTech and Moderna vaccines—and that was substantially aided by Operation Warp Speed funding—did not exist 20 years ago, and had this pandemic occurred in 2000, we might have to "make do with less effective vaccines…or wait until at least 70 percent of the population had gotten the virus.

The lessons from the 1918-1920 Spanish flu pandemic are that pandemics have an impact on the economy but so do interventionist government policies. During the Spanish flu pandemic, the Federal Reserve pumped money into an economy that still had many features of the war economy in place, after World War I, including boards controlling industries and high tax rates. James

Grant detailed in his book, *The Forgotten Depression* how this condition led to a Depression and double-digit unemployment. The situation today is similar, with the Federal Reserve pumping out money including stimulus checks, a depression resulted because of state and federal government interventionist policies. A Federal Reserve Bank of New York study about the Pandemic of 1918 noted, "First, the pandemic leads to a sharp and persistent fall in real economic activity. We find negative effects on manufacturing activity, the stock of durable goods, and bank assets, which suggests that the pandemic depresses economic activity through both supply and demand-side effects. Second, cities that implemented more rapid and forceful non-pharmaceutical health interventions do not experience worse downturns."[19]

The recovery from the 1920-21 depression came as result when Harding administration moved toward austerity accompanied by tax cuts and budget cuts plus tariff. The recovery came in the second half of 1921. (Many economists would argue that Harding's tariffs were not a boost to recovery but an obstacle.) We have seen how to recover from deep recessions or depressions, and it begins with free market policies. Research by Lee H. Ohanian, an economist at the University of California (Los Angeles), shows the government interventionist polices of Herbert Hoover caused the Great Depression and Franklin Roosevelt's policies in his first term delayed recovery as the unemployment rate never went below 10 percent in the 1930's, rising to 19 percent in the recession of 1937-38. About Hoover's policies, Lee H. Ohanian "concludes that the Depression is the consequence of government programs and policies, including those of Hoover, that increased labor's ability to raise wages above their competitive levels. The Depression would have been much less severe in the absence of Hoover's program." Ohanian added, "Presidents Hoover and Roosevelt shared similar goals of fostering industrial collusion and increasing real wages and raising labor's bargaining power. Hoover accomplished these goals during a period of deflation by inducing industry to maintain nominal wages, and by promoting and signing legislation that facilitated union organization and that increased wages above competitive levels, including the Davis-Bacon Act and the Norris-LaGuardia Act. Roosevelt accomplished these goals with the NIRA and the Wagner Act, both of which raised wages well above competitive levels while increasing industrial collusion." [20]

Other theories about what caused the Great Depression included the Federal Reserve tightening money and contributing to deflation and Hoover's implementing tax increases and increasing government spending. Hoover signed the Smoot-Hawley tariff in which sent tariffs even higher and set the stage for a trade war that choked off international trade at the worst point of the Great Depression. (Republicans raised tariffs during the 1920's, but Harding and Coolidge lowered taxes and cut the federal budget. Hoover ended up raising taxes to go with higher tariffs *and* increased federal spending.)

Hoover's intervention in the economy led to the great Depression. Harold B. Cole and Lee H. Ohanian added, "There are two striking aspects of the recovery from the Great Depression in the United States: the recovery was very weak and real wages in several sectors rose significantly above trend. These data contrast sharply with neoclassical theory, which predicts a strong recovery with low wages." [21]

FDR's loose monetary policy helped but many of the New Deal programs delayed recovery throughout the decades as output never matched what was seen before the Great Depression, going into World War II. The Obama recovery of 2009-17 paled in comparison to the Reagan recovery of 1982-89 even though unemployment was slightly higher at the beginning of the Reagan recession than the Obama recession.

Biden administration economic proposals feature far more government interventionist policies than at any point since the 1930s and are essentially socialistic. These policies are to the left of what even Obama proposed. The key to economic recovery will be removal of the present government policies imposed by the states that are stunting economic growth, and the hope that the Biden administration will not pursue interventionist policies in the economy You need a private sector to grow to reignite the economy. Just as Reagan and one example was Reagan approach which unleashed the private sector and ensured nearly 20 years of economic growth. *The Democrats' idea of raising minimum wages and imposing the Green New Deal will not only suffocate the recovery but may end up causing a long economic downturn that will last for years.*

The biggest lesson that should be learned from the pandemic is that human ingenuity when unleashed can go a long way to solve problems whether it is finding new life saving uses for off-the-shelf drugs or new tests that can detect the coronavirus in five minutes. Operation Warp Speed saw the development of vaccines in the United States and in Great Britain in record time. Our long-term recovery begins when we recognize that free men and women can rise above the COVID-19 crisis and reinvent our country and our planet.

The longer the shutdown continues, the worse our prospects will be. George Mason University economist Donald J. Boudreaux and Alberto Mingardi, a political scientist at Italy's IULM University, wrote, "Today, though, rather than trying to stimulate activity in the wake of the pandemic, governments are aiming to stop it. And at this task, everyone must agree, governments are performing splendidly... Once the coronavirus is under control, restarting the economy faces many obstacles—especially social distancing. If we continue to remain at arms' length from one another, we will hamper our natural 'propensity to truck, barter, and exchange,' identified by Adam Smith as a key source of economic growth." [22]

The challenge to policymakers after the pandemic is to restart an economy even though many of its features have already disappeared. An economy based on secure property rights along with free markets, can recover quickly if market prices are not regulated and producers' ability freedom? to profit are allowed. The strategy during the pandemic was the complete opposite as many businesses are told not to produce and are restricted in not just how to produce, but even what they are allowed to produce.

The Biden administration's proposals will make matters worse because they will try to control the economy from Washington expanding on how governors such as Gretchen Whitmer in Michigan, Tim Walz in Minnesota, Gavin Newsom in California, and Andrew Cuomo in New York are doing in the states. The Green New Deal supported by the administration is not about saving the planet but is designed to transform the economy beginning with telling utility companies what energy sources they will use, what kind of automobile you can drive, how large your home will be, and how long the fossil fuel industry will be permitted to exist. Raising the minimum wage beyond what the market will support ensures that many on the bottom of the economic ladder will not get jobs or rehired. Fifteen dollars an hour is a far higher wage than many states can support. Small businesses that struggled to survive the pandemics will not survive the increase of the minimum wage to 15 dollars an hour. In addition, "green" policies such as encouraging high-density population centers and increased public transportation are the same policies that lead to quickest spread of the virus.

Democratic governors have shown that *they have moved beyond regulating businesses but also regulating how individuals behave.* While some recommendations—wearing masks, encouraging social distancing—make sense others are simply overkill just as Michigan outlawing planting gardens in the early part of the pandemic. We have dealt with these issues with our report, *The Pursuit of Economic Growth*, as we detailed a series of goals and ideas to spread the economic growth through the middle class and the cities. We called for a series of reforms that would help create an entrepreneur class to go with an investor class. We also called for tax reforms, budget reforms and policies that would advance liberalized trade.

Several principles for a future recovery must be adhered to. The first principles, as stated by Donald J. Boudreaux and Alberto Mingardi, are: "What we need is not more fuel pumped into the GDP machine but assurances that its internal processes aren't blocked. Governments have purposefully stopped the economy. To get it moving again, we eventually must remove obstacles that keep individuals from participating in market processes, both as consumers and as specialized producers."[23] The Democrats' continued insistence of seeking stimulus and propping up blue state inefficient governments will only slow down any recovery just as Obama's stimulus slowed down his recovery. Obama is the only President since Herbert Hoover to have any year where the economy did not grow at least three percent.

The recession of 2020 began with the stock market plummeting, putting our ideas of expanding the investor class in jeopardy. Our plans to create an entrepreneur class our threatened by the business-killing shutdowns imposed by many governors. We need to open up the economy and be rid of obstacles that will prevent many businesses from restarting. As I wrote about Democrats' economic theory in 2017, "What is missing from this formula is the creation of wealth. How often during the 2012 election did we hear from Obama or Senator Warren that entrepreneurs didn't build their business, but government did through the creation of roads and schools; entrepreneurs and business merely were inventions of government policies." [24]I added, about Democrats' economic theory, "What is missing from this formula is the creation of wealth. How often during the 2012 election did we hear from Obama or Senator Warren that entrepreneurs didn't build their business, but government did through the creation of roads and schools; entrepreneurs and business merely where inventions of government policies as oppose to being created by entrepreneurs themselves. Businesses, say the democratic socialists, are to be servant of the government, contributing to what the government deems necessary... all of economics is a zero-sum game in which a producer of underarm deodorants are stealing food from hungry children and government must step in to guide businesses in the right direction while taking from the wealthy to share with the Middle Class and the poor." [25]

We may see at least three trillion dollars deficits as a result of this crisis, proving my thesis "that government positive policies will benefit an economy on the margins, if it allows the private sector to function and innovate. The ability of bad government policies to do great harm is massive." [26]As Donald J. Boudreaux and Alberto Mingardi noted, *"Today, though, rather than trying to stimulate activity in the wake of the pandemic, governments are aiming to stop it. And at this task, everyone must agree, governments are performing splendidly."*[27]

Government policies can be a blunt object and that blunt instrument has closed the economy and sent millions of people unemployed. When this is over, the lockdown will be seen as the worst mistake made in a generation. What is missing is a plan to restart the economy, and while it is easy to stop an economy in its place, it is even harder to restart one and be rid of the government obstacles shackling the economy in place.

Matt Ridley observed that the British government put many obstacles in place after World War II, "Three years after the second world war ended, the government was still micromanaging the decisions of consumers. Incredibly, it was nine years of peace before rationing ceased altogether. Bread was rationed for the first time in 1946, potatoes in 1947. Only then did the slow liberalisation of shopping begin. Flour was derationed in 1948, clothes in 1949, petrol, soap, dried fruit, chocolate biscuits, treacle, syrup, jellies and mincemeat in 1950, tea in 1952, sweets in 1953, cheese and meat in 1954. The black market thrived."[28]

The goals begin with getting our economy started by opening the economy and overcoming the difficulty of running an economy in a pandemic. The 1918-1920 pandemic came on the heel of a nation saddled with government obstacles, including war boards design to run the economy, nationalized railroads and high tax rates to pay for the war, as well as a Federal Reserve that first expanded monetary policy, producing inflation, which was followed by a depression with unemployment that may have reached 12%. The recovery began when the economy was liberated, and the pandemic eventually ended.

There was a V-shaped economic recovery in 2020, but as the pandemic surged at the end of 2020, the recovery appeared to stall and the total number of those employed dipped in December. *This stalled economy was the direct result of state governors delaying recovery.* Any further stalled economy will be fault of the governors who restricted growth and Federal government policies *that were about redistributing wealth as opposed to creating wealth.* The right policy can produce a lasting recovery beginning with lowering the tax rates on businesses and individuals combined with removing the cap on upper income limits to the social security and Medicare tax (FICA) tax, which would raise taxes on the wealthy. We showed that if you lower FICA taxes by 1% and removed the income cap, it would raise $90 billion per year.

We talk about dealing the budget in our report, "The other part is what we already mention that we need to review both spending and regulations. Trump administration efforts to deregulate the economy are showing some benefit and regrowth by reducing the government impact upon the economy. On the budget side, no one can disagree that spending has substantially increased." [29]

To restart the economy, we need to review both spending and regulations. The Trump administration's efforts to deregulate the economy showed benefit and regrowth by reducing government's impact upon the economy. Spending has substantially increased and there is very little stomach at this point to reform entitlements. Indeed, Democrats want to *expand* entitlements including "Medicare For All, universal child allowances, and making community colleges free, The best strategy may be to review spending either by restoring the sequester the Republicans forced Obama to accept to reduce the growth of spending the growth of spending or simply start reviewing departments and look for either elimination or cutbacks at places like the Department of Energy, especially since the fracking revolution has made the department obsolete.

Eventually, entitlement reforms will be needed, but until the economy recovers, we can look for cuts in the present budget, where there is plenty to cut or reduce. *Eliminating or reducing departments will not only cut the budget but in many cases, be important in reducing regulations which produce obstacles to growth.*

Much of Main Street and rural America has provided the core of the Trump coalition, but they are ones being squeezed in the economic shutdown and lockdowns. CNBC host Jim Cramer observed, "the stock market is rising as big business rebounds from state-ordered stoppage of nonessential activity, while small businesses drop like flies."[30] In 2009, the Tea Party began as a protest against the Troubled Asset Relief Program (TARP) favoring massive federal bailouts to big corporations. Tea Party supporters both supported keeping federal government spending in line with a populist view that government favored big business as the expense of small businesses.

Joel Kotkin has been warning for years about a coming feudalism in which the middle class is being squeezed. Kotkin warned, "Ultimately the shift of millennials to the Left could lead to a conflict between the oligarchs and the clerisy over the appropriation of wealth. *The way things look now, the battle will be over who pays for an ever-expanding welfare state—not how to expand the middle class.* This is likely to shift our politics increasingly in an authoritarian direction. As the great historian Barrington Moore noted, 'No bourgeois, no democracy.' In a country where the middle ranks are shrinking, the elites more powerful, and ideological polarization is on the rise, the prospects for democracy, even in its greatest homeland, could be grim indeed...*In the world envisioned by the oligarchs and the clerisy, the poor and much of the middle class are destined to become more dependent on the state. This dependency could be accelerated as their labor is devalued both by policy hostile to the industrial economy, and by the greater implementation of automation and artificial intelligence.*" [31]

The left is already moving toward a statist populist political strategy that will in the end strengthen government control over our lives. If Republicans don't come up with their own plan to strengthen the middle class, much of what remains of the middle class will move to the left. Kotkin's point reinforces what I have stated earlier, that the left *and much of our political class are not interested in increasing the economic pie but redistributing what is left of our economic pie.* The Biden administration would only accelerate this pace of redistribution of wealth from the middle class to the uber rich and the oligarchy.

Another important issue is whether the United States can uncouple itself from China. This won't be as easy as many of the products we buy are manufactured there and to move them to the United States would encompass economic sacrifice, including higher prices. We will not be able to transfer all our manufacturing back to the United States or even our USMCA partners in Canada and Mexico without economic costs. While some manufacturing can be brought back home from overseas, including pharmaceuticals, we will need to find a dependable supply chain. For example. India was originally not going to export hydroxychloroquine to the United States. keeping the raw materials for the drug home for their own population but relented after a phone call to Prime Minister Narendra Modi from Trump. India stands to profit in the long run as becoming part of our supply chain, maybe replacing some of what is manufactured in China and this move may have been designed to show the rest of the world that India can be depended upon. In my book *The Rise of National Populism and Democratic Socialism, What Our Response Should Be,* I wrote, "India, for many years, has set itself apart from the West, but in recent years, this is beginning to change. Gone are the days of reflective anti-American attitudes that infiltrated Indian leadership and there is a more balanced approach to world events. It will be imperative among American policy makers to encourage India to become a permanent member of the Anglosphere." [32] About trade policies, I wrote, "Throughout our history, it was not uncommon for American presidents to seek temporary economic rehabilitation against other countries to open up trade opportunities for American goods and services. Both President Reagan and President George H.W. Bush did this, putting 'tariffs' on selected goods and industries from other countries. But their goal was to liberalize trade not to restrict it, and both presidents made sure these steps were temporary, and used as a means to open up trade and reduce barriers to American goods." [33]

Free-trade presidents have been willing to use tariffs to open up trade. The effort to decouple China will mean continuing trade troubles with the second largest economy and we will see tariffs on Chinese goods, but it does beg the question of where we go to increase our markets. Many nationalists have promoted an industrial policy and some cases an autarkic economic policy, but an industrial policy has its limitations since it puts the government in a position of picking corporate winners and losers.

We do have options beginning with expanding the USMCA to include Great Britain, New Zealand and Australia forming a giant Anglosphere trading bloc. Once the bloc if formed, we can begin negotiations with the European Union. We can add European democracies, South Korea, and Japan to the trading bloc. We may want to design strategies to help develop India as an economic counterweight to China as well as build up other nations like Indonesia as future economic partners. These moves will be closer to managed trade but if it increases trade beginning with Democratic and economically advanced nations, we may make up for disruption of China trade. This will be controversial since many populists are opposed to an agreement that would encourage more free trade but a trade agreement with a democratic alliance will not only help our economy and that of our allies, but it gives us options in dealing with China. *Any trade agreement with India will have not just economic impact but also geopolitical consequences as India's position in the Indian Ocean may be important in protecting the sea lanes and India is also has an important location that could disrupt China's Silk Road strategy to set up global infrastructure along former trading lanes of ancient times to control trade from China to the Middle East and Europe.* Another aspect may be a development of tax policies encouraging companies to move manufacturing from overseas to the United States. Trump economic advisor Larry Kudlow suggested that we should reduce corporate taxes in half for companies returning manufacturing to the United States. This may smack of industrial policy but encouraging companies to move some of their manufacturing back to the United States will aid us in decoupling from China. This policy combines of both industrial policy for selected manufacturing sectors and free trade policies with democracies from Eastern Europe to the Pacific rim including South Korea, Japan, and Australia with possible future expansion into India.

Ned Ryun of Americas Majority Foundation polled Arizona voters and found that 75% of voters would vote for a candidate running for Congress who has plans to make the United States self-sufficient in food, energy, and medicine. In Kansas' 3rd Congressional District, we asked if the US should continue to trade with China as we did before COVID-19 and work within international institutions like the World Trade Organization to enforce fair trade rules and international standards or isolate China by actively encouraging businesses to move operations out of China, return sensitive manufacturing to the U.S., crack down on Chinese industrial spying and build a coalition of nations to counter China's ambitions. Fifty-five percent of voters supported isolating China as opposed to keeping business relations unchanged and the majority of groups we surveyed agreed with only the most leftist voters supporting business as usual. Voters support an industrial policy to protect key industries. The GOP can combine free market trade policies with our allies to go with selected protection of key businesses Senator Tom Cotton recommended areas for protection including Pharmaceuticals, personal protective equipment, and machine tools, which Tom Cotton noted were important to our public health and industrial production. The long-term goal is to preserve free markets while ensuring that not only are key businesses are protected but most of the trade is liberalized, and we strengthen our alliance against China not just militarily but also economically.

The cost of the COVID recession could prove greater than the virus itself. For every one percent reduction in the GDP will produce a 3.3 percent increase in drug overdoses and nearly a one percent increase in suicides. This data comes from *The Lancet* and the National Bureau of Economic Research. Dr. Jonathan Each added this, "The state of our economy is not just a monetary risk, it is a health risk. When people lose their jobs, they typically lose their health insurance. The *British Journal of Psychiatry* found that there were more than 10,000 'economic suicides' because of the 2008 recession. Similarly, a 2016 study from *The Lancet* found that there were an excess 260,000 cancer deaths associated with the recession. These statistics also fail to mention the increased domestic violence, increased child abuse and home loss when schools and businesses are closed."[34]

The unemployed and under-employed will suffer the consequences and they are the forgotten Americans who paying the price for lockdowns. It is not a case of "open up the economy and people die" since more people likely will die from the jobs lost from the economic downturn than from the disease. It is about making sure if there is an American economy left to return to after the pandemic. Models that predicted massive deaths if lockdowns were imposed have been shown to be flawed and we are basing economic decisions on these models. Many models have been changed numerous times within a period to reflect new data but some of the original models greatly overestimated the deaths and hospitalizations COVID-19 caused.

Among the things we should from the pandemic:

1. Pandemics by themselves damage the economy and this pandemic would have reduced or eliminated economic growth even without the severe damage lockdowns caused. In hindsight, we could have done what the Swedes did, keep

the economy open and reduced the damage done to the economy. Great Barrington Declaration emphasized the need to target and protect the most vulnerable including our seniors and those with underlying conditions.

2. Conservatives need to understand that the left will use this crisis to further their own goals of transforming America into a "democratic socialist" state. Joe Biden has moved to the left and will be a mere puppet in his own administration, controlled by the socialist wing of the Party.

3. We need to make the case that free market ideas are the best way to speed the recovery quickly and have our own game plan to do exactly that including tax plans, budget plans, and ideas on both trade and regulations that both grow the economy and reduce government.

4. China has shown itself to be a threat and we need to design new alliances to counter this threat along with trade policies that strengthen our ties with our democratic allies throughout the world.

5. Many within our own country, including the media have allowed their own economic interest to cloud their judgment about China.

6. Finally, we should design plans to ensure that we will be ready for the next pandemic *and hold China responsible for this one.*

Ronald Reagan summed up its best, "Freedom is never more than one generation away from extinction. We didn't pass it to our children in the bloodstream. It must be fought for and handed on for them to do the same, or one day we will spend our sunset years telling our children and our children's children what it was once like in the United States where men were free."

Economic Ideas

I n a study, we reviewed the current base of the conservative coalition as we wrote "The hard-working Middle class and many
of them are facing a retirement crisis including 35% of working
Republicans over the age of 50 who are likely to face an income
shortfall in retirement. These are the people most likely to have
to stop working younger due to health reasons and most likely to
depend on Social Security for retirement income. Cutting Social
Security or delaying payment of full retirement benefits hits the
base of the Conservative Coalition very hard. In our survey among
senior voters, a third of Republicans along with two thirds of independents supported taxing the wealthy to ensure Social Security
solvency and even add additional benefits. To understand the
retirement crisis, it helps to look at how it plays out at the individual level. A 55-year-old currently making $50,000 year could
expect to receive $1,090 a month if they started taking Social
Security at age 62 or $1,600 a month if they waited to age 67. If
this person has $100,000 saved by age 67 and expects to live to 80,
they can reasonably plan to draw $8773 in monthly income from
their retirement savings for an annual income of about $30,000
(before taxes) if they can wait till age 67 to draw Social Security. If
this same person has to retire at 62 due to a health problem and
has $85,000 saved, their monthly income from Social Security and
savings drops to $1,678 a month or $20,000 a year." [35]

Polling by VCreek/AMG has found that more than 40% of retirees with savings of less than $100,000 retired because of a health problem or downsizing and that includes 35% of Republicans over the age of 50. [36] The impact of the retirement crisis could dramatically realign the electorate, as a significant share of those who would be hit the hardest are members of the current Trump/Conservative coalition. The Social Security Trustees currently estimate the Social Security Trust Fund will be depleted in 2035, which will likely necessitate a cut in benefits. The Democrats have already proposed their plan the "Social Security 2100 Act," which includes phrasing out the $132,000 cap on Social Security taxes and increased rates to fund increased payments to retirees. The Republican Study Committee has advocated a plan that would not raise taxes and extend the life of Social Security by realigning "full retirement age to account for increases in life expectancy since the program's creation" by gradually increasing "the normal retirement age at a rate of three months per year until it reaches 69 for those reaching age 62 in 2030." [37]

The Republican plan would also make adjustments to encourage seniors to stay in the labor force longer and increase payments for workers who had lower lifetime earnings. Both the Democrat and Republican plans are actuarially sound. The Republican plan, though accurate in terms of life expectancy, does not account for working longevity. People may be living longer, but their productive working years have not increased at the same rate as their lives have. The people most likely to need Social Security earlier because health problems reduce their capacity for work are more likely to have lower savings, lower life-time earnings and have engaged in blue collar or skilled trades work—the types of workers who are currently forming the base of the Conservative coalition. The Democrat plan with its tax increases does not take into the account the secondary effect that taxes have on the economy by reducing monetary elasticity.

Historically, higher tax rates coincide with more frequent recessions. Recessions and their associated drops in the stock market wipe out the retirement savings of the middle and working classes and in terms of jobs tend hit the working classes that form the base of the conservative coalition the hardest. The main tax paid by working Americans earning less than $200,000 a year is the Social Security payroll tax.

Most Americans Pay More in Payroll Taxes Than in Income Taxes

Percentage of Taxpayers with Greater Payroll Taxes than Income Taxes, 2019 (Projected)

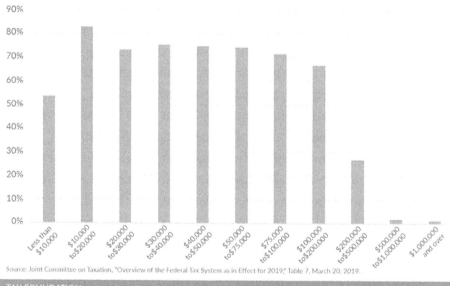

Source: Joint Committee on Taxation, "Overview of the Federal Tax System as in Effect for 2019," Table 7, March 20, 2019.

TAX FOUNDATION @TaxFoundation

Among all the taxes, Social Security is the most accepted by the voting public because they understand the direct benefit they will receive. Everyone pays into the program and everyone knows several people who benefit from it, which is why it is regarded as a fair tax. The goal is this research project to start a conversation among conservatives about the framework of a plan that is actuarially sound, accounts for the realities of working careers and the rates at which older workers retire due to health reasons, reduces taxes on the middle class, extends the life of the Social Security Trust Fund into the next century and does not drag on the economy by increasing the overall tax burden and its associated effects on monetary elasticity. It also uses supply side economics to expand multifactor productivity. We believe we have found a middle ground to start the conversation. If you lower Social Security tax by one percentage point, the break-even point to be revenue neutral is raising the cap on the maximum income subject to Social Security taxes to $168,000 and if you eliminate the cap totally, you will add $88 billion per year and close to $1.7 trillion dollars of revenue to Social Security over 20 years. The Trump economy begins with reducing tax rates across the board, reducing regulations, and reducing the impact of the administrative state. It is not just the amount of money sloshing around in the economy that creates growth, but the freedom to do something productive with the money free from regulations. Our proposal is simple: reduce the tax burdens upon the middle class by cutting the payroll tax rate while extending its reach and allowing for more production in the economy through other income tax and corporate tax reforms. We also call for cutting regulations and reducing unnecessary spending on agencies and programs that have outlived their usefulness. The goal is to provide a stable safety net for those in need while allowing for opportunities to succeed. Our plan is a small first step toward the policy deliberations needed to build a coalition to extend Social Security and expand economic productivity.

New Economic Ideas

In the Americas Majority Foundation study, *Taxes and Social Security in the New Paradigm*, we described the current state of the conservative coalition: "The hard-working Middle class and many of them are facing a retirement crisis including 35% of working Republicans over the age of 50 who are likely to face an income shortfall in retirement. These are the people most likely to have to stop working younger due to health reasons and most likely to depend on Social Security for retirement income. Cutting Social Security or delaying payment of full retirement benefits hits the base of the Conservative Coalition very hard. In our survey among Senior voters, a third of Republicans along with two thirds of independents supported taxing the wealthy to ensure Social Security solvency and even add additional benefits. To understand the retirement crisis, it helps to look at how it plays out at the individual level. A 55-year-old currently making $50,000 year could expect to receive $1,090 a month if they started taking Social Security at age 62 or $1,600 a month if they waited to age 67. If this person has $100,000 saved by age 67 and expects to live to 80, they can reasonably plan to draw $8773 in monthly income from their retirement savings for an annual income of about $30,000 (before taxes) if they can wait till age 67 to draw Social Security. If this same person must retire at due to a health problem at 62 and has $85,000 saved, their monthly income from Social Security and savings drops to $1,678 a month or $20,000 a year."[38]

Polling by VCreek/AMG has found that more than 40% of retirees with savings of less than $100,000 retired because of a health problem or downsizing and that includes 35% of Republicans over the age of 50.[39] The retirement crisis could dramatically realign the electorate, as a significant share of those who would be hit the hardest by shortfalls in retirement income are part of the current Trump/Conservative coalition. The Social Security Trustees currently estimate the Social Security Trust Fund will be depleted in 2035, which will likely necessitate a cut in benefits. The Democrats have proposed their plan, the Social Security 2100 Act, which includes phasing out the $132,000 income cap on Social Security payroll taxes and increased payroll tax rates to fund increased payments to retirees. The Republican Study Committee has advocated a plan that would not raise taxes and extend the life of Social Security by realigning "full retirement age to account for increases in life expectancy since the program's creation" by gradually increasing "the normal retirement age at a rate of three months per year until it reaches 69 for those reaching age 62 in 2030." [40]

The Republican Study Committee plan would also adjust and encourage seniors to stay in the labor force longer and increase payments for workers who had lower lifetime earnings before their retirement. Both the Democratic and Republican plans are actuarially sound. The Republican plan, though accurately forecasting life expectancy, does not account for the number of years people work. People may be living longer, but their productive working years have not increased at the same rate of life expectancy has. The people most likely to need Social Security earlier because health problems reduce their capacity for work are more likely to have lower savings, lower life-time earnings and likely work in blue collar or skilled trades—in short, the types of workers who are the core of the conservative coalition. The Democrats plan with its tax increases does not take into the account the secondary effect that taxes have on the economy by reducing monetary elasticity.

Historically, higher tax rates coincide with more frequent recessions. Recessions and their associated drops in the stock market wipe out the retirement savings of the middle and working classes and in terms of jobs tend hit the working classes—the base of the Conservative Coalition— the hardest. The main tax paid by working Americans earning less than $200,000 a year is the Social Security payroll tax.

In the United States, since World War II, as tax rates have gone down, recessions have become less frequent. Many on the left have no problem with personal income tax rates as high as 70% or even 90% and view the 1950's and 60's as a golden era in which the top income tax rate ranged from 70% to 90%. While the 1950's were a decade of prosperity, there were four recessions from 1948 through 1961, when the tax rates at 90% and overall growth was only 2.3% through the decade, which was one half of the Reagan decade.

The 1960's boom was as much due to supply side economics on the tax side as President Kennedy's economic team dropped tax rates down from 90% to 70% and at the end of the decade, Lyndon Johnson added a 10% income tax surcharge combined with increased spending for both beginning of the Great Society and funding the Vietnam War led to a recession in 1970. The Kennedy tax plans later provided a model for the Reagan tax cuts in the 1980's, which led to over two decades of prosperity interrupted by brief recessions in 1991 and 2001.

The decades of the 70's saw both rise of inflation and three recessions before the Reagan policies took full effect at the end of 1982, leading to nearly a quarter of a century of growth. From 1969 to 1982, we saw three recessions including the 1973-5 recession, which saw unemployment peak at 9%, and the 1981-2 recession which unemployment peaked at 10.8% (which exceeded the recession of 2007-2009 with an unemployment peak of 10.1%.).

The world has changed since the Reagan years. In 1979, the highest income tax rate was 70% and many in the middle class were forced into higher tax brackets and seeing much of their gains disappearing due to high tax rates. Today, the top income tax rate is 37% and many middle class people either don't pay income tax or pay very little income tax. but the biggest tax for the middle class is the payroll tax. From 1988 to today, the top income tax rates ranged from 28% to 39% and from the 1980's through the 1990's policies included stable monetary policies, lower tax rates and lower capital gain taxes. Budget growth was restrained through various deals, including the Rudman-Gramm-Hollings deal of 1985 and the Newt Gingrich-Bill Clinton budget deal in 1997. These compromises led to widespread prosperity, with all classes—families, minorities, high school graduates, college graduates—seeing their incomes rise. These rising incomes led to a rise in the investor class, as new saving vehicles such as IRAs allowed the middle class to save for their future and increase their retirement nest egg. The impact of recessions on retirement savings is devastating which makes sustained productivity growth paramount. If a recession overlaps with the 2035 Social Security shortfall, retirees, and workers over 50 could never recover their losses.

Among all the taxes, Social Security is the most accepted by voters because they understand the direct benefit they will receive. Everyone pays into the program, and everyone knows several people who benefit from it. Therefore Social Security is regarded as a fair tax. The goal in this chapter is to start a conversation among conservatives about creating a Social Security plan that is actuarially sound, accounts for the realities of how long people work as well as the rates at which older workers retire due to health reasons, reduces taxes on the middle class, extends the life of the

Social Security Trust Fund into the next century and does not drag on the economy by increasing the overall tax burden and its associated effects on monetary elasticity and uses supply side economics to expand multifactor productivity.

We believe we have found a middle ground to start this conversation. If you lower the Social Security payroll tax by one percentage point, the revenue-neutral break-even point is raising the cap on the maximum income taxed for Social Security to $168,000. If you eliminate the maximum income cap totally, you will add $88 billion per year and close to $1.7 trillion of revenue to Social Security over 20 years. Our proposal reduces the tax burdens on the middle class by cutting the payroll tax rate while extending the reach of income taxed and allowing for more production in the economy through other income tax and corporate tax reforms, cutting regulations and reducing unnecessary spending on agencies and programs that have outlived their usefulness. The goal is to provide a stable safety net for those in need while allowing everyone opportunities to succeed. Our plan is a small first step toward the policy deliberations needed to build a coalition to extend Social Security and improve economic productivity.

The Current Economic Paradigm

Many conservatives can't see how the economy and the demographics of the country have changed since the Reagan era. Many conservatives in economic solutions appropriate for 1985, when tax rates were higher, broad-based domestic manufacturing still employed large percentages of the population and there was less pressure from international economic competition. Until very recently, working class and middle-class wages have been flat due in part because productivity has been flat. Only recently in the 2019 has multi-factor productivity increased. A growing share of U.S. exports are software, patent licenses, platforms, and consulting services. The growth of these companies does not necessarily create more jobs. A tax cut for owners of these companies may not lead to investments and expansion of their businesses that improve productivity and create rising wages for the middle and working classes. As Harvard Business Professor Thales Teixeira has noted, many of fastest growing companies are not disrupting market segments by creating new products but by disrupting the customer value chain, creating a more seamless service through a scalable platform. Middle skill jobs and lower skill blue-collar jobs that create enough value to produce high wages have been decreasing. The skilled trades that do pay well require skill levels and conscientiousness that are often above the range of the traditional factory worker.

The manufacturing conducted in the U.S. is large, durable, highly precise, expensive equipment, energy or highly customized consumer goods. Pressuring manufacturing productivity further is the collegization of education. By directing more and more middle-class students to college, industry and trades are being deprived of a pool of conscientious workers who can perform at a high level of skill producing large, durable, highly precise equipment. These young people who in past decades would not have gone to college then often start careers with student loan debt and low value creating white-collar jobs, giving life to the economic phenomenon of "bullshit jobs."

These people don't want an income tax cut; they want a pay raise and meaningful work. To understand this in action, let's look at a married couple with $80,000 in wages using the 2020 1040-EZ. After the standard deduction they have $55,200 in taxable income. According to the 2020 tax tables they pay $7,940 in tax, an effective rate of 9.95% of gross. Cutting their effective rate by 1 point to 8.95% reduces their tax burden to $7,160 a year or 8.04 percent. They experience that as $16.75 per individual paycheck *if* the payroll reductions are properly adjusted. The variable nature of income taxes with deductions, exemptions and credits means a small tax cut may not provide any fiscal benefit to a worker paying a low effective tax rate. As discussed, we have not seen income tax rates exceed 39% and for many Americans the biggest federal tax is the payroll tax, not the Federal income tax.

For Americans earning up to $200,000 dollars the number one tax is the payroll tax. For the same workers in the example above, their Social Security Tax is $9,920. Most companies are sophisticated enough to build the "employer's half" into total compensation accounting. The employer paying half is a fiction. The employee pays it all.

Reducing the Social Security rate by one point cuts this couple's payroll taxes to $9,120, saving them $800, which they will experience as $16.66 per individual paycheck. Because the Social Security payroll tax is not subject to variation, it is a near certainty that the worker will have extra money in their regular paycheck. What workers really want are regular pay increases created by rising productivity. If their pay increases by 2% they are up $1,600. If it increases year over year at 2% for 10 years their joint income is $97,000, a gain of $17,000. The income tax cuts only saved them $8,000 over the same period. With the ability of 401k plans to step up savings rates with pay raises, the income gain puts this couple on a stronger footing for a secure retirement. By 2007, 63% of Americans had investment savings but a decade after the 2007-2009 recession that number dropped to 53%. *That showed that not only did income stagnate, but also overall wealth declined.*

As unemployment dropped in the past few years and more companies offered 401k plans, participation in investment savings has climbed. Polling we commissioned by VCreek/AMG finds that 57% of people in the private economy have some type of retirement savings plan.[41] These people's retirement savings have been buoyed by record high stock market valuations. A reduction in the Social Security payroll tax for workers is the most direct way to deliver direct, visible, tax relief. The per-paycheck amount is not large, but across tens of millions of workers the economic effect on the economy could be massive. All business activity is ultimately about something an individual consumer purchase. A payroll tax cut is the most direct way to inject purchasing power into the economy. And supply side economics is more than just increasing the amount of money in the system; it is about creating dynamism in the system. I wrote in my book, *The Rise of National Populism and Democratic Socialism: What Our Response Should Be,* "We are affected by a shrinking private sector compared to an ever-expanding federal government. In the past Republicans have talked about tax cuts, but it is time for a review of what supply side economics means in a nation with $20 trillion dollars in debts and where a half trillion-dollar deficit in a fiscal year is considered a minor miracle…It is time to rediscover the supply side of economics and expand upon it. In the past, economic conservatives have concentrated on taxes but not on spending. The Heritage Foundation over the past two decades has rated countries by economic freedom. The foundation concluded that countries with the highest rating for overall economic freedom were often the most prosperous and equally important, most were politically free. The Heritage ratings didn't just include taxes but also national budgets, regulations, how easy it was to start a business, and how open these countries were to trade." [42]

A reduction in the Social Security payroll tax for workers needs to be seen as part of a larger economic strategy that reduces regulatory friction and government debt service that drag on the economy. Today the economic environment has changed, and many Conservative Coalition voters no longer view income tax cuts by themselves as the magic bullet. Our own research has shown that many Republicans support higher taxes to fund expansion of Social Security. In our survey among senior voters, a third of Republicans along with two thirds of independents supported taxing the wealthy to ensure Social Security solvency and even add additional benefits.

The Democratic left has already made it clear that they are prepared to expand government services from health care to Social Security and to pay for it, they will raise taxes on the middle class. Their model is supposedly the Nordic countries, where the middle classes pay substantially higher taxes either through value added or payroll taxes. Nordic countries have retreated from their more leftist policies over the past two decades and it was only in 2017 that the United States finally reduced their corporate tax rates to be competitive with the Nordic countries The Democratic left has already made it clear that they are prepared to expand government services from health care to Social Security and to pay for it, they will raise taxes on the middle class. Their model is supposedly the Nordic countries, where the middle classes pay substantially higher taxes either through value added or payroll taxes. Nordic countries have retreated from their more leftist policies over the past two decades and it was only in 2017 that the United States finally reduced their corporate tax rates to be competitive with the Nordic countries. The Biden plan will raise corporate tax rates to 28% and with state taxes included, will raise the overall corporate tax rates to 32%, among the highest in the developed nations.

Make America Mediocre Again: Biden's Corporate-Tax Agenda

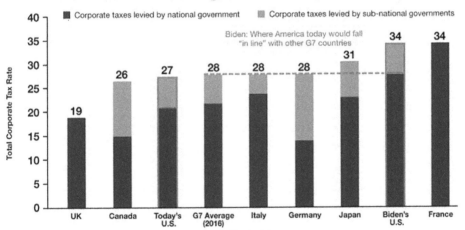

Notes: The UK and France have zero sub-national corporate tax rates. All units are in percentage points. All country-level tax rates shown are statutory tax rates for calendar year 2019. Source: OECD; author's calculations.

NR | CAPITALMATTERS

The Democrat-sponsored Social Security 2100 Act would raise the payroll tax from the present 12.4% to 14.8% plus eliminate the cap on taxable income, which adds to the tax burden on the wealthy. This plan appeals to broad portions of the electorate. Part of this is due to many seniors retiring with nest eggs of $100,000 or less, not being fully prepared for their retirement and that many seniors are forced to retire either due to health reasons or downsizing, thus not be able to add to their wealth. The conservative coalition needs a plan that considers the new paradigm and political realities.

The Americas Majority Foundation has entered into this debate with a paper on lowering payroll tax rates. The foundation worked with the Center of the American Experiment researchers John Phelan and Mitch Rolling to review the consequences of different ways of changing the payroll tax. We asked the researchers to address two main questions:

A. How much revenue would be lost from Social Security revenues if the payroll tax rate were cut by one or two percentage points?

B. How much would the earnings limit have to increase by to be revenue neutral if the payroll tax rate was lowered?

Methods incorporated included using the top 15% of incomes as a base for the earnings limit, so the researchers could determine how many tax returns would have had to pay more payroll taxes the earnings limit been raised – for example, an additional 10% of tax returns would have had to pay more if the earnings limit was capped at what the top five percent paid and an additional 5% when matching the top 10%.

(All Values In Billions)	2017	2016	2015
Total Earnings	$8,375.55	$8,020.50	$7,817.70
Total Taxable Earnings	$6,983.38	$6,662.80	$6,484.10
Effective Earnings Covered	83.4%	83.1%	82.9%
Actual Tax Revenue	$873.60	$836.20	$794.89
Set Tax Rate	12.40%	12.40%	12.40%
Effective Tax Rate	12.51%	12.55%	12.26%

As the chart below shows, lowering the Social Security payroll tax rate by one or two percent would have reduced tax revenue in 2015-2017 of $201.3 billion for a one percent tax cut and $402.61 billion for a two percent cut, unless the taxable earnings limit was eliminated entirely in both scenarios.

(IF 1% LOWER)				
(All Values In Billions)	2017	2016	2015	Total
Effective Tax Rate	11.51%	11.55%	11.26%	
Tax Revenue	$803.77	$769.57	$730.05	$2,303.39
EXCESS/DEFICIENCY	($69.83)	($66.63)	($64.84)	($201.30)
Raise CAP To 90%				
Total Taxable Earnings	$7,538.00	$7,218.45	$7,035.93	
Tax Revenue	$867.60	$833.75	$792.18	$2,493.53
EXCESS/DEFICIENCY	($6.00)	($2.45)	($2.71)	($11.16)
Eliminate CAP				
Total Taxable Earnings	$8,375.55	$8,020.50	$7,817.70	
Tax Revenue	$964.00	$926.39	$880.20	$2,770.59
EXCESS/DEFICIENCY	$90.40	$90.19	$85.31	$265.90

(IF 2% LOWER)				
(All Values In Billions)	2017	2016	2015	Total
Effective Tax Rate	10.51%	10.55%	10.26%	
Tax Revenue	$733.93	$702.94	$665.21	$2,102.09
EXCESS/DEFICIENCY	($139.67)	($133.26)	($129.68)	($402.61)
Raise CAP To 90%				
Total Taxable Earnings	$7,538.00	$7,218.45	$7,035.93	
Tax Revenue	$792.22	$761.57	$721.82	$2,275.61
EXCESS/DEFICIENCY	($81.38)	($74.63)	($73.07)	($229.08)
Eliminate CAP				
Total Taxable Earnings	$8,375.55	$8,020.50	$7,817.70	
Tax Revenue	$880.25	$846.19	$802.03	$2,528.46
EXCESS/DEFICIENCY	$6.65	$9.99	$7.13	$23.76

2. Raising the taxable earnings limit to cover 90% of all earnings would have almost entirely recovered the losses of lowering the tax rate by one percent, leaving a deficiency of only $11.16 billion from 2015-2017. For a two percent payroll tax cut, a raise in the taxable earnings cap to 90 percent of all earnings would have still left a tax revenue shortfall of $229 billion from 2015-2017. Eliminating the earnings limit and implementing a payroll tax cut

of one percentage point would have added an additional $265.9 billion in taxes from 2015-2017. Eliminating the earnings limit and implementing a two percent cut in payroll taxes would have added $23.76 billion in 2015-2017. Because a two percent payroll tax cut would require the elimination of the earnings limit to be revenue neutral, our study looked more closely at a one percent payroll tax cut, which would require a rise in the earnings limit to at least 90% of taxable earnings to reach this 90 percent level, the limit in 2015 and 2016 should have been somewhere around $166,000- $168,000, instead of the $118,500 earnings limit in those years, or an increase of more than 42 percent.

	Tax Returns	Top 1%	Top 3%	Top 5%	Top 10%	Top 20%	Top 25%	Earnings Limit	In Between 20% & 10%
2015	141,204,625	$480,930.00	$253,979.00	$195,778.00	$138,031.00	$93,212.00	$79,655.00	$118,500	$115,621.50
2016	140,888,785	$480,804.00	$256,673.00	$197,651.00	$139,713.00	$94,620.00	$80,921.00	$118,500	$117,166.50

Since $168,000 represent the break-even point for the cap to match up with the revenues raised with a one percent payroll tax cut, we can assume that any earnings limit higher than $168,000 will raise more taxes than the present tax collected at the lower cap. So should the earnings limit be raised or eliminated? Eliminating the earnings limit in 2015-17 would have raised an average of $88 billion in those years and an additional $1.8 trillion dollars of additional payroll taxes over a 20-year period.[43].

The overall tax reduction for the middle class with one percent would be approximately $500 for those with annual earnings of $50,000 or close to $2,000 for earnings of $200,000. This would add to the nearly $1,400 that the average American earned from the first wave of Trump's tax cuts. While Biden has claimed that his tax plan will only tax the rich, the reality is that much of the middle class will be wiped out from new taxes. As we mentioned already, the Democrats' Social Security 2100 plan will increase middle class taxes substantially.

What will happen to the upper and middle classes if the cap on Social Security taxation is eliminated? We will review the question of the effect of cap elimination on other taxes in a future study. Since Social Security payroll taxes are dedicated to the program payroll tax increases could be offset by lower marginal income tax rates on higher earners or adjustments to capital gains, investment income or pass-through business income taxes. The goal of the reductions in payroll taxes on higher earners would be to spur capital reinvestment, thus increasing productivity.

The current Republican Social Security plan, though actuarially sound, does not match the reality of how long older workers will remain in the labor force and is thus unlikely to be politically feasible. The current base of the Conservative Coalition is made up of workers who are the least prepared for retirement and most likely to need Social Security for retirement income due to having to end their working lives due to a health problem. Large shares of Republican and independent voters are open to an increase in Social Security taxes and the program is extremely popular. We want to start a conversation about the best rates for Social Security payroll taxes as part of a larger conservative plan for economic growth that addresses reduced regulation and discretionary spending, and lower business taxes and income taxes.

The Tax Foundation's John Olson observed, "Payroll taxes are a highly effective way to raise revenue, for three main reasons: First, the payroll tax base is very broad. Payroll taxes apply to all wages and salaries up to a cap of $118,500, which nearly 83% of wages and salaries fall under. Furthermore, unlike the personal income tax, payroll taxes do not include dozens of deductions, exemptions, and credits that narrow the tax base. This means that payroll taxes can raise a large amount of revenue at a relatively low rate, to the tune of over $1 trillion a year...Second, due to the inelasticity of the supply of labor, payroll taxes generate a comparatively small amount of deadweight loss compared to other forms of taxation. This means that payroll taxes lead to a relatively small amount of economic inefficiency, since the quantity of labor in the market does not dramatically decline as a result. Overall, payroll taxes do much less economic harm than taxes on capital. This is evidenced by our analysis of Senator Bernie Sanders' tax proposals, whose payroll tax rate increase raised nearly four times as much revenue as his proposed increases on capital gains and dividends, but with a fourth less of the impact on GDP…Finally, payroll taxes are very hard to evade. According to the IRS' criminal enforcement data, investigations into payroll tax abuse make up less than 3 percent of all tax investigations, despite payroll taxes generating about a third of all federal tax revenue." [44]

Olson's view is that overall burden of eliminating the Social Security payroll tax cap would have not severely damage the economy but still cause some harm. Lowering the payroll tax rate would be a middle-class tax cut that most voters could see and present an alternative to the Democratic plan that includes raising the payroll tax. Republicans can now not only present a fair tax that would be less regressive but also, as Olson noted, "Furthermore, this additional revenue could be used to lower marginal rates on corporate and personal income, growing both wages and GDP by 2.2%, while still raising revenue." Republicans can present a plan that is growth oriented while lowering taxes for all Americans. But this would be the first part of a plan that includes plans to review both spending and regulations.

The Trump administration's efforts to deregulate the economy showed benefit and were pro-growth by reducing the government impact on the economy. On the budget side, spending has substantially increased and there is very little stomach at this point to reform entitlements. Democrats want to expand entitlements including "Medicare-For All that would expand entitlements to almost all Americans as a prelude for exploding the welfare state. The best strategy may be to review spending either by repeating what Republicans did in the Obama administration when they forced Obama to accept sequesters to reduce the growth of spending and/or or simply start reviewing departments to eliminate them or cut them back. For example, why should there be a Department of Energy, since the fracking revolution has made the Department obsolete? As for entitlements, no reform will come until there is a bipartisan agreement, and many Republicans are no more willing to cut entitlements than Independents or Democrats.

Many Republicans will not support any reductions in Social Security and with 25% of Americans retiring before age 65 for health reasons and another 8% retired due to job downsizing, it will be difficult to convince Americans to support an increase in retirement age to collect benefits even if the increase takes place over decades. Lowering payroll taxes by one percentage point will give middle class taxpayers an additional tax cut and provide a sharp contrast to the Democratic plans which mandate a massive tax increase for the middle class. The Social Security 2100 Act includes a 2.4% tax increase for the middle class[45]

When Colorado and Vermont calculated the cost of imposing Medicare for All statewide, legislators determined the cost to the middle class was a additional 10% to 11.5% rise in the payroll tax. Sen.' Bernie Sanders acknowledged in the Democratic presidential debate on June 27, 2019, that imposing Medicare for All would require a massive tax increase for the middle class. While Biden has denied that he will support a "Medicare for all", the "public option" supported by a majority of Democratic members of Congress is a Trojan horse for Medicare for All. *So, the Democrats' plan for Social Security and Medicare For All means a massive tax increase for the Middle Class.*

Republicans should base their economic reforms on the following principles:

1. Lowering the Social Security payroll tax by one percentage point and increasing the maximum income cap beyond $168,000. Eliminating the cap totally would add an additional $88 billion per year of extra revenues.
2. Lower corporate and marginal tax rates to encourage economic growth.
3. Continue to reform regulations to reduce the cost these regulations impose on individuals and businesses.
4. Review each federal department for possible cuts and consider a sequester on the Federal budget to begin controlling spending. This proposal allows for the middle class to receive a tax cut, while ensuring that Social Security remains sustainable. A growth-oriented tax plan combined it with regulatory reforms and budget restraints will allow growth to continue and redefine supply side economics to encompass more than just taxes.

The Voter Population

N ational Populism and democratic socialism look like fresh solutions compared to the nearly half of decade of rhetoric of mainline Republican and Democrat Socialism. They have a root in the same place: *a low growth economy in the US, stagnant wages, flat productivity growth* resulting from the Industrial Revolutions having matured and the U.S. having to compete against every other country in the world. The big difference between Democrat Socialism and National Populism in their narrative is brand positioning. We need a narrative to understand the world and we look for villains and heroes, while assuming there are victims. JD Johannes and I observed, "National Populism and Democratic Socialism have almost the same story plotlines, but different characters to fill the roles. National Populism appeals to people who hold traditional values—Patriotism, the dignity of hard work, respect of Christian faith and the value of traditional family roles. The values University of Illinois Professor Andrew Hartman described as, "values that middle-class whites recognized as their own."[46] In the National Populist narrative, the victims are people who work hard and follow the traditional values of the middle class. The villains are a vague Establishment and various "losers" who have rigged or screwed up the system so much, following the rules no longer works." Trump's supporters viewed Trump as a hero for standing up to the establishment in his effort to restore American greatness. During the 2016 primary, Trump's own coalition was a broad one that included the very conservative, in the center and some moderate Republicans, evangelicals, and small businessmen. These voters were ready to for a message that took their concerns seriously while not mocking their values. JD Johannes and I noted, "National Populism benefits workers in industries the government favors for protected status, businesses who cannot sustain foreign competition, companies holding government backed debt, and companies willing to collude with the government for business advantages. Democratic Socialism appeals to people who hold Progressive values—Multi-Culturalism, Social Justice, equality of outcomes, a belief that smarter technocrats can create a more just world and spiritualism in place of religion." [47]

For the Democratic Socialists, everyone is a victim except white men who have rigged the system to benefit themselves. These democratic socialists have aligned themselves with many within the corporate communities and tech oligarchies have provided both funding for the Democratic Socialists' agenda and censoring conservative voices on social medias.

The risks and dangers of National Populism is the perception that many within the movement no longer believes Republican leadership take their values seriously. They take as evidence leaders such as Rep. Liz Cheney supporting Trump's impeachment, even though that support ultimately led to her losing her leadership position. When Liz Cheney said during the second impeachment, *"I'm also concerned we have to stand up. I owe you the truth, I owe my constituents the truth, you owe us the truth, we all owe each other that, and the truth is: **We cannot become the party of QAnon, we cannot become the party of Holocaust denial, we cannot become the party of white supremacy."* [48] Power Line blogger Paul Mirengoff wrote, "The Republican Party is not the party of QAnon, Holocaust denial, or white supremacy. It is in no danger of becoming that party...The claim that the GOP may be veering in that direction is a Democrat/mainstream media talking point. Cheney should not be espousing it." [49] Mirengoff's point is to warn that if Liz Cheney and others within the leadership of the Republican Party continue this path, they will push a significant portion of the Trump coalition out of the Republican Party and if this occurs, Cheney's own desire to return the Republicans to a majority status as the defender of free markets will be closed.

There's a strong possibility that a third of Trump voters could easily walk out the door. How do you replace these many voters? You can't. This loss would be a leftist dream come true, creating a political landscape in which conservatives and libertarians will be moved to the sidelines and the possibility of a Populist third party that can't win but yet at the same time, keep the Republicans from winning. France is where the future of the populist movement lies if a portion of the Republican leadership and a few never-Trumpers succeed in "removing the stain" of Trump from the GOP. Marine Le Pen is not a traditional American conservative or even a believer in the free market. Many of Le Pen's views mirror the hard left, embodied by Jean-Luc Melenchon, a leftist with close, strong ties to the French Communist Party. including her promise in the last French presidential election to maintain the 35-hour work week (with overtime forbidden) and lowering the retirement age to 60. (The two combined collected 42% of the vote in first round voting showing political strength of their ideas.) Le Pen's populism moved her to the left and present President Emmanuel Macron; a former member of the Socialist Party, campaigned to the right of Le Pen on economic issues.

Marco Respinti noted, "The phenomenon of allegedly "far-Right" organizations trying to be not unknown in the United States. Conversely Lyndon LaRouche, a onetime Marxist (of French heritage, no less), "breached into the Right" by aligning his movement with Liberty Lobby and anti-Semitic organizations in the 1970s and '80s. Plus ça change, plus c'est la même chose…Perhaps the undertaking is less an example of politically opportunism than a recognition of ideological kinship." [50] Le Pen's National Rally party's economic plan that she campaigned on in 2017 began with a 35% tax for any French companies that produce their goods outside of France and her goal is a "reconquest" of French markets with policies moving toward economic autarky—French goods produced by French workers. Marine Le Pen would add a tax of 10% to a foreign worker's salary, including citizens of European Union countries.

Le Pen's economic policies moved to the left, not to the right, and there is no reason why a populist third Party in the United States wouldn't move to left on the economic policies, preventing free market defenders from having an opportunity to victory.

Le Pen's complaints about the EU have merit since the since the EU has become a bureaucratic nightmare, attempting to run the economies of European nations including immigration policy by forcing nations to accept refugees from the Middle East after the chaos erupting as the result of the United States removal of Libyan dictator Muammar Gaddafi, the Syrian civil war, and the rise of ISIS. The EU showed it was perfectly willing to dispense with democratic niceties if it interfered with the EU agenda. In June 2017, the EU threatened to take action against the Czech Republic, Poland and Hungary for refusing to take their share of refugees from the Middle East. The EU failed to inoculate their population against the coronavirus as quickly as compared to Great Britain and the United States. They failed to secure enough supply contracts even though one of the best vaccines was developed by the German firm BioNTech and distributed throughout the world by Pfizer.

Le Pen's anticapitalism is hardly a basis for a successful economic policy. What Le Pen is a big government nationalist who will use government largesse to benefit her supporters. Le Pen's policies are what could happen in the United States if Trump supporters believe their views are ignored by the Democrats' monopoly of government control, a developed populist movement that could drag 35% of Republicans and a high percentage of Sanders' supporters into a national populist big government party. If that happens, Liberty will die a slow death. Rasmussen found that 53% of Republicans would leave the GOP for a third party led by Donald Trump and 72% of Republicans view Trump as the model for what their party should stand for.[51]

Over the past several years, we have reviewed the Trump coalition. We concluded, in 2017, "Americans are facing a retirement crisis including 35% of working Republicans over the age of 50. A poll commissioned by the Transamerica Center for Retirement Studies and by Harris Poll found that 30% percent of Baby Boomers (age 55-73) have less than $100,000 in retirement savings and 45% percent of Generation X (age 41-54) have less than $100,000 in retirement savings. There is rich data on emerging trends of retirement preparation however most polls about retirement savings and readiness do not ask questions about partisan political identification and ideological world view."[52] Nearly half of people we surveyed confirmed they were living comfortably and only 14% viewed themselves as struggling but the real question centers on 39% of those "getting by." How many of this group is one major illness away from "getting by" to "struggling" and how do they define a "safety net"?

Republicans without a college degree account for 73% of Republican workers over age 50 who have saved less than $100,000. The average retirement savings for a college graduate over age 50 is $154,000. In 2016, only 17% of workers had an employer-sponsored pension plan so in the last three decades, retirement shifted from being an employer obligation to a worker responsibility. To make up for this preparation gap many planned on working in retirement. Transamerica finds that 57% of people with some college or less plan on working in retirement. The disastrous pandemic lockdown slipped the economy into a deep recession. that hurt blue-collar workers, lower-income workers, and minorities. Far too many small businesses and Main Street businesses closed, leading to the lower class losing their jobs while many in the upper class saw their incomes rise. Unemployment and economic hardship were most profound in Democratic run states, where the harshest lockdowns occurred.

Another recession would also likely cause a marked decline in the size of retirement nest eggs. Liberals and Progressives are positioning themselves to take advantage of this crisis with proposals to increase Social Security payments funded by an income tax increase and allowing workers over the age of 50 to "buy in" to Medicare for health insurance. Both proposals are popular even with voters who identify as Republican.

We commissioned three polling firms to conduct surveys for this project. We found a strong relationship between education and retirement preparation.

1. A significant share of Republicans supports increased Social Security benefits, paid for by tax increases on the rich.
2. A significant percentage of Republicans think individual workers should have less responsibility for paying for their retirement than they do today.

A large share of Republican supports expanded Medicare benefits from "Buy In" for supplemental benefits to "No out-of-pocket expenses" (no co-pay) and the growing "divide that explains American politics" also illuminates this retirement crisis.

For many higher-income, college educated voters, there is no retirement crisis. The Trump/Conservative coalition, whose significant base of support are people who did not graduate from college. are open to Liberal/Progressive ideas on resolving the retirement crisis. As we have seen, many of the Trump coalition are struggling economically.

There is a strong impression among voters, including many Trump voters, that wages and salaries are not keeping up with expenses and that they are just treading water financially. Debt, particularly student loan debt, and the costs of health care and health insurance, which rises faster than inflation, takes a huge portion of workers' earnings.

The challenge for Republicans is to protect their base among older voters, while designing a strategy that appeals to voters ages 18-49 and college graduates. Younger voters are facing their own financial distress with student loan debt that could slow down their accumulation of wealth for retirement. For older voters, conservatives are lacking policy solutions that focus on looming challenges to retirement savings and health care costs. In addition to addressing Social Security issues, *conservatives need to emphasize economic growth not only as a key for full employment but as an absolute necessity for maintaining and increasing retirement savings.* The number of voters willing to increase taxes on the wealthy as a solution to shore up and even increase Social Security benefits is something conservatives must understand and deal with. Seniors will not allow their own benefits to decline in any future budget crunch. They feel entitled to the benefits of both Social Security and Medicare because they have been contributing to the system for all their working lives.

Viewing Socialism

To a slim plurality of voters, the word 'Socialism' does not mean a dictatorship of the proletariat seizing the means of production. In fact, many voters, Republican and Democrat, simultaneously hold positive views of socialism and capitalism simultaneously.

We surveyed voters in 2019 how they view the terms "socialism" and "capitalism." On socialism, we asked, "When you hear or read the term 'socialism', do you think of Scandinavian Social Democracies like Denmark and Sweden OR Venezuela, North Korea and the Former Soviet Union?" On capitalism, we asked, "When you hear or read the phrase 'free market capitalism do you think…It is an economic system that allows people to pursue their passions and create their own careers and businesses or do you think It is an economic system where those at the top benefit at the expense of the rest." Our goal was to understand the prism through which these voters they view both socialism and capitalism.

Fifty-two percent of all respondents associate "socialism" with "Denmark/Sweden." Simultaneously, 52% define "Free Market Capitalism" as being able to "pursue their passions." Sixty-seven percent of Democrats think "Denmark/Sweden" when they hear the word "socialism." When Democrats hear the term "free market capitalism" 64% respond "it is an economic system where those at the top benefit at the expense of the rest." For Republicans, the numbers are essentially reversed. Democrats associate socialism with the Scandinavian countries that have robust welfare states and "social democracy." Republicans view socialism as what is happening in Venezuela, where the society has totally collapsed into massive poverty. These results are not surprising.

capitalism by party

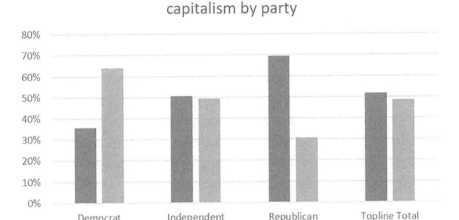

Capitalism Pursue Passions   Capitalism Top Benefit

What is more intriguing is understanding that among the 52% who associate "socialism" with "Denmark/Sweden" more than half also associate "free market capitalism" with "an economic system that allows people to pursue their passions and create their own careers and businesses?" A full 27% of respondents answered their support offing favor of both Nordic social democracies *and* free market capitalism. It should be noted that Denmark and Sweden are indeed free market Democracies. Among the Democrats who answered "Denmark/Sweden" when explaining their support for socialism, a full 40% also associated capitalism with pursuing their passions. These Democrats' embrace of socialism is not about a dictatorship of the proletariat seizing the means of production, it is more likely a desire for a robust health care and social services safety net. Highly visible factions of the Democratic Party have moved sharply to the left and many are now openly socialists and Bernie Sanders is not the only one willing to admit his socialistic views. Many of the Democratic proposals are even more to the left than what many Scandinavian politicians would propose.

Many Republicans and quite a few independents view socialism as a failed economic system. A key feature of our future may be how Americans view socialism and capitalism. If Americans decide the values that undergird the Scandinavian view of social democracy as the path they want, the Democrats win, and many Americans do view capitalism as a system that benefits the elite one percenters and not ordinary workers.[53]

In a report for Americas Majority Foundation, we wrote, "The U.S. is still a country where wealth and income earned through hard work and personal risk taking is respected. Our national survey in 2014 found interesting dynamics. 71% of Blacks, 79% of Whites and 66% of Hispanics believe that hard work is still rewarded but when asked if the economic system rigged against the Middle Class, we see the results reverse. 71% of Blacks, 65% of Whites and 61% of Hispanics believe the economic system is rigged. In a survey among Michigan voters in August of 2016, two of every three voters viewed the system rigged against the Middle Class with two/thirds of White and Black voters along with 55% of Hispanic voters viewing the system as being rigged against Middle Class. Even with that cynicism, four out of five Michigan voters believe that to increase economic opportunity and a fair opportunity to succeed, you must grow the private sector, which is the position taken by Republican candidate Donald Trump, the first Republican who won Michigan since 1988." [54]

Many Americans are of two minds. They think that hard work is still rewarded and support the proven principles of productive work, delayed gratification and personal responsibility *and* they also fear that the system is rigged against them. They see a system where hard work doesn't help you climb to the top; a system where time-honored principles don't lead you to a better life than your parents had. While they respect entrepreneurs, who startup companies and create jobs, they have less respect for executives who manage long-established companies. The heart of the complaint is deals with executives who are paid millions while seemingly running great enterprises— General Electric. JC Penney, Sears—into the ground. And who artificially prop up the value of their stocks through. A more sophisticated version of the complaint is buoying stock valuations through buy backs.

This entrepreneur/manager divide is part of the explanation on whether a person sees capitalism as a system that allows people to pursue their passions or a system where only the elites benefit. If they see capitalism as a system where CEOs win and everyone else loses, they will likely think of it as rigged. If they see capitalism as a place where entrepreneurs can succeed. They are more likely to think of capitalism as a system where people can pursue their passions. If voters see capitalism as providing opportunities for entrepreneurs, they are more likely to think of capitalism terms of pursuing passions.

Drilling down into party affiliations in our polls reveals some partisan trends, the lack of economic agreement inside the parties and the challenges and paths to forging a prevailing view voters have about economics. The policy divergences among Democratic presidential primary contenders and fissures in the Democrats House majority are likely a product of 40% of self-identifying Democrats being socialist sympathizers and the other three types not yet aligning to form a majority coalition. The unifying force among Democrats may not be policy as much as their opposition to President Trump— who is no longer president. What is clear though, despite activist rhetoric, many of rank-and-file Democrats are not sold on true Marxist socialism.

The GOP has divergences yet has formed a policy agreement around an opposition to Socialism with President Trump showing a commitment to the concerns of "populists capitalists" who have not fared well under previous trade agreements and are concerned about the consequences of illegal immigration. Independents are nearly equally distributed among the Economic View Typologies. Beyond the perceptions of "Socialism" and "Capitalism" there is agreement on the importance of hard work and personal responsibility.

VCreek/AMG asked respondents "To what extent do you agree or disagree with the following statement 'hard work, delayed gratification and taking personal responsibility are important to make our society work.'" A topline 88% strongly or somewhat agree the proven principles "are important to make our society work." Among respondents who answered "Denmark/Sweden" 42% strongly agreed the proven principles are important. Even 39% of the "Socialist Sympathizers" strongly agree!

As indicated by the poll results, the average reasonable voter accepts the proven principles of achieving excellence through hard work. These voters do not necessarily understand that the extreme progressive left that makes up the base of "socialist sympathizers" is attacking the proven principles. For example, University of Pennsylvania law professor Amy Wax was vilified by progressives for an op-ed, written with her law school colleague Larry Alexander, that argued that the proven principles work for individuals, the economy and society. Wax and Alexander wrote, "That culture laid out the script we all were supposed to follow: Get married before you have children and strive to stay married for their sake. Get the education you need for gainful employment, work hard, and avoid idleness. Go the extra mile for your employer or client. Be a patriot, ready to serve the country. Be neighborly, civic-minded, and charitable. Avoid coarse language in public." [55]

Respect authority. Eschew substance abuse and crime. These basic cultural precepts reigned from the late 1940s to the mid-1960s. They could be followed by people of all backgrounds and abilities, especially when backed up by almost universal endorsement. Adherence to these principles was a major contributor to the productivity, educational gains, and social coherence of that period. To most Americans, Wax's statement is a simple endorsement of the basic rules to getting ahead in life. But after publication of the op-ed in the *Philadelphia Inquirer* there were calls for the University of Pennsylvania to fire Wax. Her fellow professors also condemned her.

The average reasonable voter working hard, busy living their life by the proven principles is unaware that there is a substantial political movement that sees these principles as repugnant. In forming a winning coalition around a prevailing policy or economic agreement, voters need to understand that there is a group that opposes their beliefs, and that the opposition group is substantial The path to victory for the Trump/conservative coalition could be to defend and promote capitalism as a system that allows people to pursue their passions against those who disparage the proven principles combined with a commitment to a robust health care safety net and deliberate actions to control the costs of health care. President Trump seems to understand this. He campaigned in 2016 on the issue and took deliberate executive actions to control the costs of health care. Polling by Pew found that the economy and health care costs were voter's priorities for President Trump' and Congress in 2019. Health care and the economy go together for voters because health insurance premiums are a significant expenditure for most voters and health care costs are the most significant unknown financial risk. The Nordic countries, whether

most voters truly understand it or not, are able to finance gen-
erous public health care benefits through a dynamic capitalist, free-
market economy and culture built on the proven principles. As the
New York Times reported, *"the endurance of the Nordic model has
long depended on two crucial elements — the public's willingness to
pay some of the highest taxes on earth, and the understanding that
everyone is supposed to work."* (Emphasis added) [56]

A free market, capitalist economy that allows people to pursue
their passions through the proven principles is the most viable path
to reducing the financial burden of health insurance premiums
and finance a risk-reducing health care safety net in a country
with the size and complexity of the United States. But the socialist
sympathizers don't want a system where people can pursue their
passions and they think people who live and support the proven
principles are the problem. Their path leads not to Nordic capitalism but to Venezuelan socialism.

Does free market capitalism create great prosperity and allow
millions to escape poverty. or does free market capitalism benefit those at the top at the expense at the rest. We found that 76%
of Democrats agreed that free market capitalism benefitted the
rich at the expense at the rest whereas 88% of Republicans and
63% of independents viewed the free market as good, creating
great prosperity for millions. Overall, 62% of retirees favor the
free market as being good and benefitting millions while creating
prosperity. Seventy-five percent of voters who see themselves as
leftists disagreed with the notion that the free market is good
and believed that markets exploit the masses, while 88% who
view the world from the right believe that free markets are good
for prosperity.

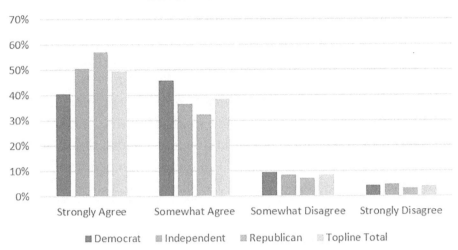

The conservative coalition must define what socialism really means and that Socialism is *not* Nordic capitalism. Warren, Sanders, "The Squad" and the media are selling Denmark/Sweden, but their policies are not Nordic capitalism. Occasionally the truth slips out. Saikat Chakrabarti, the retired chief of staff of Alexandra Ocasio-Cortez (and her political guru) stated about the Green New Deal, "The interesting thing about the Green New Deal...it wasn't originally a climate thing at all... Because we really think of it as a how-do-you-change-the entire-economy thing." [57]

Ocasio-Cortez and her ilk are interested in complete transformation of our economy and society into a socialist paradise, far beyond anything taking place in the Nordic countries. As we will show, much of the Democratic proposals are beyond the Nordic countries, but then Bernie Sanders admits he is a socialist and many of his opponents voting record are not much different than his nor are their proposals significantly different than what he is proposing. In fact, what Sanders, Elizabeth Warren and others on the Socialist Left are proposing start to mirror the populist, anti-free-market agenda of France's Marine Le Pen.

Marine Le Pen is a warning to American conservatives that the populism of people who think Capitalism is a system where only the top benefit could easily turn left. Elizabeth Warren's economic plan proposed during the 2020 primaries is nothing more than leftwing populism, comparable to what Le Pen is selling the French voters and what Peron sold Argentina. In that regard, Joe Biden has become the Marine Le Pen of American politics when it comes to economic policies. He has allowed Elizabeth Warrens, Bernie Sanders, and Alexandra Ocasio-Cortez to set the agenda for his administration.

Instead of educating voters on what Socialism really is, it may be easier to show what Nordic Capitalism really is. Nordic Capitalism is built on business freedom, free markets, private property and a culture of work that values the proven principles.

In a report by JP Morgan, Michael Cembalest reviewed the Nordic countries and found that Nordic countries are hardly socialistic even though they do have a robust welfare state. Cembalest noted, "On many measures, the Nordic approach to the private sector is even more business friendly than the US."[58] That includes business freedom, starting new businesses, property rights protection, and free trade. Cembalest added, "Another sign that Nordic countries are not following a democratic socialist model: Nordic 'state control' is not much different from US levels. As part of its assessment of competitive Nordic Capitalism, the OECD analyzes the extent of state control and government regulation. One method shows that Nordic governments exercise even less state control over the economy than the US, while another shows that over time, government regulation affecting competition in critical network sectors in Nordic countries has converged to US levels. Either way, it's clear from this data that the state control principles of democratic socialism (i.e., replacing private ownership with collective ownership of the means of production) are very much at odds with the Nordic free-market model."[59] On tax policies, Nordic corporate and income tax rates are not much different than the United States, especially if you combined many State income taxes in the United States along with the Federal income tax rates.

Cembalest noted, "Note how corporate taxes contribute just 2%-3% of GDP in both the Nordics and the US, and how little Nordic countries rely on taxing capital gains of individuals, regardless of income levels. Finally, some Nordic estate tax rates are actually zero, with an average of 11% compared to US estate tax rates of 40%." The Nordic countries' biggest taxes are through VAT's and payroll taxes and much of this is hit the Middle Class. The Nordic countries do spend more on the welfare state, but their economy is dependent upon not killing the golden goose that support the system, the private sector. Michael Cembalest observed "With Nordic countries firmly rooted in capitalism and free markets, if I wanted to find examples of democratic socialism in practice, I'd have to look elsewhere. I broadened my search and looked for countries that, relative to the US, are characterized by:

1. Higher personal and corporate tax rates, and higher government spending
2. More worker protections restricting the ability of companies to hire and fire, and less flexibility for companies to set wages based on worker productivity and/or to hire foreign labor.
3. More reliance on regulation, more constraints on real estate development, more anti-trust enforcement and more state intervention in product markets; and a shift away from a shareholder-centric business model
4. More protections for workers and domestic industries through tariff and non-tariff barriers, and more constraints

on capital inflows and outflows. I couldn't find any country that ticked all these democratic socialist boxes, but I did find one that came close: Argentina, which has defaulted 7 times since its independence in 1816, which has seen the largest relative standard of living decline in the world since 1900, and which is on the brink of political and economic chaos again in 2019." [60]

The Democrat economic model is closer to Peronist Argentina, a country that since the days of Juan Peron is closer to a corporatist model than a free market model. At the turn of the twentieth century, Argentina was one of the richest countries in the world, but it has slipped behind other nations.

David Sirota, a speechwriter and senior adviser for Bernie Sanders's 2020 presidential campaign, wrote in Salon in 2013, "Chavez racked up an economic record that a legacy-obsessed American president could only dream of achieving. the Venezuelan socialism "suddenly looks like a threat to the corporate capitalism, especially when said country has valuable oil resources that global powerhouses like the United States rely on." [61] Sirota's ideas are the standard for the Democratic Party.

In the journal *Democracy*, a 2013 seminar featured, "Middle Out Middle," discusses on how the left views the economy today. Eric Liu and Nick Hanauer note, "*Middle-out economics argues that national prosperity does not trickle down from wealthy businesspeople or corporations; rather, it flows in a virtuous cycle that starts with a thriving middle class. Middle-out economics demands a systemic policy focus on the skills, capacities, and income of the middle-class.*" [62] Investment and capital formation are not mentioned, but for Elizabeth Warren, Barack Obama and Hillary Clinton give money to the middle class and magically wealth is created. The question of where we get the money before giving it to the middle class is never discussed. As Liu and Hanauer write, "*Demand from the middle class- not tax cuts for the wealthy- is what drives a virtuous cycle and job growth and prosperity... Rich businesspeople are not the primary job creators, middle-class customers are; the more the middle class can buy, the more jobs we'll create...Middle-out economics means investing in the health, education, infrastructure, and purchasing power of the middle class.*" [63]

What is missing from this formula is the *creation* of wealth. Businesses, say the democratic socialists, are to be servants of the government, contributing to what the government deems necessary. Bernie Sanders stated in 2015, "*You can't just continue growth for the sake of growth in a world in which we are struggling with climate change and all kinds of environmental problems. All right? You don't necessarily need a choice of 23 underarm spray deodorants or of 18 different pairs of sneakers when children are hungry in this country. I don't think the media appreciates the kind of stress that ordinary Americans are working on.*"[64] For Sanders, economics is a zero-sum game in which a producer of underarm deodorants steals food from hungry children and government must step in to guide businesses in the right direction while redistributing OK? income from the wealthy to give to the middle class and the poor.

While Sanders talks mostly about class, the machinery of the Democratic Party is built on activists, public sector unions along with upper income consultants who benefit from government largesse and are funded by leftist oligarchs.

The Argentine model is a far cry from Nordic capitalism and Venezuelan socialism, like all forms of socialism, has failed miserably. While Sanders today has backpedaled on his support for Venezuela and claims that the country is not the ideal democratic socialist state he envisioned now that Venezuela economy has collapsed. But Republicans must face a significant reality, many Americans, maybe even half of America view socialism as

"Denmark/Sweden." Bernie Sanders, Alexandra Cortez or even Elizabeth Warren describes their policies as similar to Denmark or Sweden when their policies are actually closer to Venezuela or, at best, Argentina. The case must be made that today the Democratic Party is the party of *Venezuelan* socialism. Don't just say "socialism," say "*Venezuelan* socialism." The economic history of the past seventy years favors Republicans and free market conservatives while the Venezuelan socialists running dominating? the Democratic Party are pushing for an agenda that is Marxist and their goals are simply to allow the government to control *all* aspects of our lives. We are not talking a debate about the extent of the safety net; we should have but a deeper discussion of what kind of society we should be. Will we move toward Venezuela and other disastrous example of socialism, or will we continue to be a free market country? The conservative coalition needs a debate about the proven principles and how they are under attack. The conservative coalition needs to harness millennial voters' affinity for pursuing their passions. When Democrats in 2020 talked of Nordic countries as their models, they are lying. Their model is more extreme and dangerous. It is to turn the United States into Venezuela.

The Left's War on Science

The pursuit of truth in science died in 2020 during the Wuhan virus outbreak. 2020 saw government agencies abandon long held principles in dealing with the pandemic and a pandemic that specifically truck the elderly while having little impact on the young— even less than flu season. We crashed the economy throughout the West and will end up killing more people and destroying more communities through lockdowns than the virus ever could. A National Bureau of Economic Research study by Duke economist Francesco Bianchi, Giada Bianchi of the Harvard Medical School, and Dongho Song of the Johns Hopkins business school, estimated that as many as 900,000 excess deaths will occur over the next 15 years as result of the economic lockdown, significantly higher than the final total of Covid's death will be.)

Bianchi, Bianchi, and Song noted, "We estimate the size of the COVID-19-related unemployment to be between 2 and 5 times larger than the typical unemployment shock, depending on race/gender, resulting in a 3.0% increase in mortality rate and a 0.5% drop in life expectancy over the next 15 years for the overall American population. We also predict that the shock will disproportionately affect African Americans and women, over a short horizon, while white men might suffer large consequences over longer horizons. These figures translate in a staggering 0.89 million additional deaths over the next 15 years." [65]

This virus killed two to four per 1000, which was more than the average of flu season for the past decade, which range from three per 10,000 in 2009 to 1.7 per thousands in 2018. While the average flu season averaged one death per 1000, we had flu pandemics that have killed at least two or three per 1000 based on infectious fatality rates including pandemics in 1957 and 1968 and the worst of all influenza pandemics, the 1918-1920 Spanish flu pandemics which killed 20 to 30 per thousand.

Dr. Anthony Fauci proved the perfect example of the collapse of the scientific class, often giving contradictory information while getting the big story about the virus totally wrong, the lethality of the virus and the disastrous lockdowns which will end up killing more people than what the lockdown would ever save.

The biggest mistake Dr. Fauci made was overestimating the lethality of the virus. In Congressional testimony in March of 2020, Dr. Fauci went from the possibility that COVID-19 virus Infectious fatality rate of .1 to a 1% mortality and emphasized that this virus was 10 times the flu. This data proved to overestimate the lethality of 4 to 5 times as the infectious fatality rate ended up between .2% and .3%. The flu season between 2010 and 2019 was .1% to .18 %with an average seasonal of .13%. This overestimation led to the lockdowns, which extended beyond the original fifteen days to continuing in many parts of the country.

Rational Ground's Len Cabrera noted, "Dr. Fauci was specifically asked if COVID was less lethal than H1N1 or SARS. Rather than refer to his own NEJM (New England Journal of Medicine) article saying SARS had a case fatality rate of 9-10% (3 to 10 times worse than COVID), Dr. Fauci said, "Absolutely not... the 2009 pandemic of H1N1 was even less lethal than regular flu... this is a really serious problem that we have to take seriously." He repeated that COVID's "mortality is 10 times that [of influenza]" and concluded with, "We have to stay ahead of the game in preventing this." ...After Dr. Fauci's testimony, the "10 times more lethal" line was echoed throughout the media (see Reuters, Bloomberg, CNBC, or The Hill). A month later, the WHO was quoting Dr. Fauci's 10-times-deadlier claim. As of September 8, even the preeminent Johns Hopkins Health System still refers to COVID-19 being 10 times more lethal than flu."[66]

As data continued to stream in, 80% of deaths came from people 65 and over, which was 16 percent of the population. Many of these individuals had as many as 4.5 contributory factors. Covid-19 was not dangerous to young healthy people.

Dr. Fauci cited WHO's three percent confirmed fatality rate and shortly he promoted a national shutdown. (Remember when the country was to be shut down for 15 days to "flatten the curve">). Len Cabrera added, "After that, he was pushing for national shutdown ("15 days to flatten the curve"). This was not the strategy of isolating sick people suggested in the NEJM paper but isolating everyone. Florida's original emergency order (20-51) twice referenced a CDC recommendation for "voluntary home isolation *when individuals are sick*," (emphasis added), but then everyone was presumed to be sick (asymptomatic), and everyone was locked down (in violation of Florida Statute 381.00315, which was invoked by the emergency order)...After the two weeks to "slow the spread," [67]

Dr. Fauci used the discredited model of the University of Washington's Institute for Health Metric and Evaluation (IHME) to extend the lockdown.[68] On April 1, 2020, Dr. Fauci said we could not relax restrictions until there are "no new cases, no deaths." [69] Using poor models that overestimated the virus lethality and depending upon impossible goals such as "no new cases and no deaths" ensured the creation of bad policies that shut down the economy and resulted in massive unemployment.

Dr. Jay Bhattacharya noted, "In March, only the small fraction of infected people who got sick and went to the hospital were identified as cases. But the majority of people who are infected by COVID have very mild symptoms or no symptoms at all. These people weren't identified in the early days, which resulted in a highly misleading fatality rate. And that is what drove public policy. Even worse, it continues to sow fear and panic, because the perception of too many people about COVID is frozen in the misleading data from March." [70]

The skeptics just as Dr. Bhattacharya questioned the continued use of lockdowns and felt they were more damaging to our country than the virus. As Dr. Bhattacharya noted, "The widespread lockdowns that have been adopted in response to COVID are unprecedented—lockdowns have never before been tried as a method of disease control. Nor were these lockdowns part of the original plan. The initial rationale for lockdowns was that slowing the spread of the disease would prevent hospitals from being overwhelmed. It became clear before long that this was not a worry: in the U.S. and in most of the world, hospitals were never at risk of being overwhelmed. Yet the lockdowns were kept in place, and this is turning out to have deadly effects." [71]

The result of the restrictions: cancer patients with delayed treatment or cancer screenings not made, patients missing their diabetic monitoring, increased suicides among younger people. The economic damage added to the health issues with 130 million additional people worldwide will starve due to the lockdown's economic damage. Over the past 20 years, one billion people escaped poverty worldwide, but those gains have been threatened as economic progress has been threatened by lockdowns.

Dr. Bhattacharya and others saw in April 2020 that the actual death was significantly lower than the models as he noted, "Seroprevalence is what I worked on in the early days of the epidemic. In April, I ran a series of studies, using antibody tests, to see how many people in California's Santa Clara County, where

I live, had been infected. At the time, there were about 1,000 COVID cases that had been identified in the county, but our antibody tests found that 50,000 people had been infected—i.e., there were 50 times more infections than identified cases. This was enormously important, because it meant that the fatality rate was not three percent, but closer to 0.2 percent; not three in 100, but two in 1,000...When it came out, this Santa Clara study was controversial. But science is like that, and the way science tests controversial studies is to see if they can be replicated. And indeed, there are now 82 similar seroprevalence studies from around the world, and the median result of these 82 studies is a fatality rate of about 0.2 percent—exactly what we found in Santa Clara County...In some places, of course, the fatality rate was higher: in New York City it was more like 0.5 percent. In other places it was lower: the rate in Idaho was 0.13 percent. What this variation shows is that the fatality rate is not simply a function of how deadly a virus is. It is also a function of who gets infected and of the quality of the health care system. In the early days of the virus, our health care systems managed COVID poorly. Part of this was due to ignorance: we pursued overly aggressive treatments, for instance, such as the use of ventilators, that in retrospect might have been counterproductive. And part of it was due to negligence: in some places, we needlessly allowed a lot of people in nursing homes to get infected. But the bottom line is that the COVID fatality rate is about 0.2 percent." [72]

In the United States, for the first three and half years, of Donald Trump's presidency, those at the bottom of the economic ladder, minorities and many within the middle class saw their income rise faster than those at the top. This stopped during the lockdown.

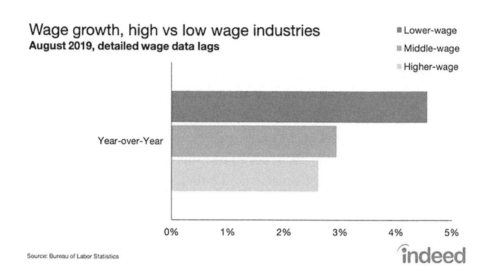

The Trump recovery before the pandemic saw many Americans, including minorities, see their income rise faster than under the Obama/Biden Administration.

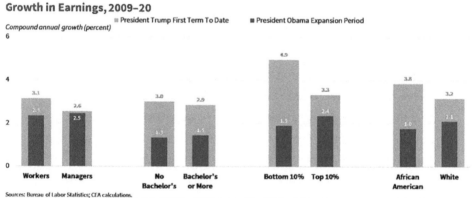

Many small businesses saw their doors shut down permanently and according to Yelp, as of September 2020, that includes 56 of every 1,000 burger places, 55 of every thousand sandwich shops, and 40 of every 1,000 gift shops.[73]. The mistakes of the lockdowns recommended by Dr. Fauci killed businesses, increased drug overdose and suicides, delayed treatment for serious illness like diabetes, heart disease and cancer, put hundreds of millions around the world at risk of starvation, and ensured schools switched to "virtual learning" that particularly hurt the poor and minorities.

While the left decries inequality, the Trump recovery *reduced* inequality by increasing wages of the middle class and the poor more significantly than the wealthy. The lockdown increased inequality, a point made by CNBC's Jim Cramer who observed that this pandemic produced the biggest transfer of wealth from the middle class and mainstream business to wealthy corporations. Many in the middle class and at the bottom saw their income drop the wealthy and while those who could work from home did all right.

As this chart showed, the rich did get richer during the pandemic and now many of these individuals are talking about resetting our capitalist system to benefit themselves even further.

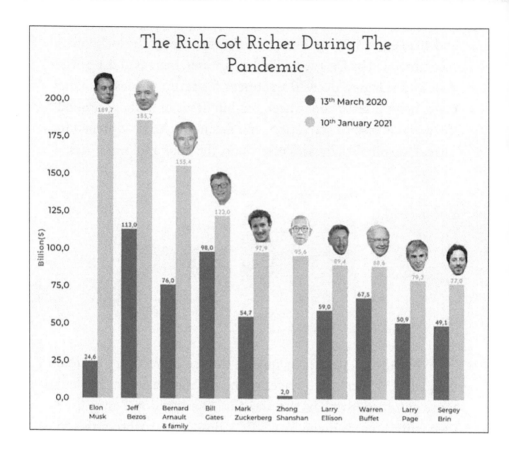

What this showed that bad science produces bad polices, economic policies in which millions saw their income dropped and millions more either died as result not of COVID-19 but of the lockdowns. Dr. Fauci's lockdown policies will end up killing more people than they will save and the bad science Fauci practices simply demonstrated how much of our scientific class not only failed policy makers, but they also shut off debate with those who disagreed with them. In doing so, Americans were denied alternatives to their plight and unfortunately for them, *the skeptics such as Dr. Jay Bhattacharya and Dr. Scott Atlas proved to be more accurate in describing both the limited harms of the virus and the problems with the solutions in dealing with the virus.*

Jordan Schachtel in his newsletter summed up this battle when he observed, "Sources in the Trump Administration, who had first-hand access to Coronavirus Task Force meetings and conversations, made it clear to me that the health bureaucrats made it their mission to destroy and delegitimize Scott Atlas, who quietly resigned from his role in late November. Sources familiar with Atlas's thought process told me that he was incredibly frustrated by the government bureaucrats' devotion to their select non pharmaceutical interventions, such as lockdowns, mask mandates, and other forms of societal and economic devastation. Atlas also remained frustrated by what could be *described as a lack of overall intellect on the task force.*"[74] He added, "Emails surfaced showing that White House Task Force members such as Birx, Fauci, Redfield, and others were enraged that Dr. Atlas came to the table with a different set of ideas, and they rightly perceived him as a threat to their monopoly on their pro-lockdown COVID messaging campaigns. Birx, for her part, routinely sent out emails through private channels to media reporters and her colleagues seeking to undermine the ideas presented by Atlas, while simultaneously refusing to defend her ideas or debate his solutions in person" [75] President Trump, who moved toward the skeptic camp, found himself fighting his own taskforce who was determined to keep economic restrictions in place. Let it be said that Trump's view of the science, like Dr. Scott Atlas, was more correct than Dr. Fauci.

The number one lesson is that lay people need not assume that the scientific class always knows what they are talking about and that their knowledge is often incomplete. Dr. Vinay Prasad reminded his fellow physicians and scientists, "Experts are not inherently smarter, more analytical, or logical than members of the lay public. Perhaps in the past, they preferentially had access to certain types of insider information. In the modern world, due to the Internet, this information gap no longer exists. This dramatically changes the game…An expert cannot distort the message to the public because too many in the public can directly interrogate the source material. In this case, that means models estimating herd immunity thresholds or the data underlying community mask use, drawing their own conclusions. If an expert seeks to distort their view of the science to further a behavioral change amongst the public, the risk of detection is high — at least by some in the public. As such, it runs the risk of immediate backlash and the ensuing loss of credibility."[76] Dr. Prasad's point should be a lesson for future public health scientists—namely, when judging their pronouncements, people can get their own information and during this pandemic, original sources were available for people doing their own research. When "experts" like Dr. Fauci contradicted themselves, their statements can easily be checked both for their earlier predictions and what science says about their track record in prediction.

Dr. Prasad added, "Once it is revealed that any individual has presented information selectively to get the listener to change their behavior — that person will forever be viewed through that lens: a calculating person. Is Fauci telling me this because the science supports it, because he believes it, or because he thinks hearing it might motivate a behavioral change on my part?…Personally, I don't see a way back from this situation. The moment the public believes that you might be withholding, selectively presenting, or distorting information to get them to behave a certain way, they will immediately put your comments through a translator."[77]

Half of America no longer believes in Dr. Anthony Fauci and the other half view him as a saint but he lost credibility as a scientist since much of what he states is viewed through a prism of politics, not science. He is the perfect example of the politicization of science where science creates "answers" that please the political class and their agenda as opposed to what the science really says. His support of the lockdown, his admiration of Andrew Cuomo and Cuomo's policies toward dealing with Covid-19 and his refusal to acknowledge the true infection fatality rate demonstrated his mistakes as well as his inability to change courses when presented with new information.

Dr. Prasad concluded with this warning: "I argued that "Follow the Science" is an incoherent message. That is because science can tell you what might happen in varying scenarios, but science cannot tell you what to value. Science is necessary for sound policy, but it is not sufficient. Humans' beings voicing their concerns and priorities, in concert with scientific guidance, is required to shape policy, and policy fundamentally belongs in the realm of politics and in the public square...This means that scientists must not distort their view of a situation to get you to do the right thing because this robs you of your ability to decide what is the right and just and virtuous course. A scientist must always and only and indefatigably tell you the scientific truth, as best they see and understand it, but we all — every one of us who votes and participates in society — we alone get to decide what the policy should be."[78] Dr. Prasad's biggest fear is being realized as the media essentially reflexively takes the side of the scientific class and the political class often the at the expense of what the science is really saying. The media also often short circuits needed scientific debate.

Hoover Institution fellow Dr. Scott Atlas, who served with the Trump Administration, notes how the media participates in the spread of scientific half-truths. "The media has done its best to misinform the public with political attacks about who is to blame for this pain and misery even as it diminishes the great achievement of the new vaccines. The decline of objectivity in journalism has been evident for years. *Now we see that even respected scientific journals, which are supposed to vet and publish the best objective research, have been contaminated by politics. Social media has become the arbiter of allowable discussion, while universities intimidate and suppress the free exchange of ideas necessary to uncover scientific truths."* [79]The media's willingness to misinform has led to unnecessary panic for a virus that killed 2-3 per 1000. The media also supported the institution of economic restrictions that will kill more people over the next two decades than the virus ever would have.

Dr. Atlas noted the stories that the media failed to cover. "The federal government also increased the protection of the elderly during late summer and fall. This effort included an intensive testing strategy for nursing-home staff and residents based on community activity, new proactive warnings to the highest-risk elderly living independently, millions of point-of-care tests and extra personal protective equipment for senior living facilities, and new alliances and financial incentives to improve nursing home infection control…The federal government also expedited development and delivery of lifesaving drugs, such as novel antibody treatments that reduce hospitalizations of high-risk elderly by more than 70%. According to HHS, more than 200,000 doses of these monoclonal-antibody drugs have been delivered to hospitals in all 50 states. Under Operation Warp Speed, the federal government took nearly all the risk away from private pharmaceutical companies and delivered highly effective vaccines, hitting all promised timelines…In this season when respiratory virus illnesses become more common and people move indoors to keep warm, many states are turning to more severe restrictions on businesses and outdoor activities. Yet empirical data from the U.S., Europe and Japan show that lockdowns do not eliminate the virus and do not stop the virus from spreading. They do, however, create extremely harmful health and social problems beyond a dramatic drop in learning, including a tripling of reported depression, skyrocketing suicidal ideation, unreported child abuse, skipped visits for cancer and other medical care." [80]

The debate over how best to deal with COVID-19 should be over, since now governors like Florida's Ron DeSantis and South Dakota's Kristi Noem have already shown that you can both protect their states' economies while seeing comparable rates in hospitalizations and deaths compared to the lockdown states.

Economists will talk of tradeoffs when discussing policies, if you do X, Y can occur and is Y a worse alternative or are you better off with not doing X? We failed this basic economic test as the path we chose failed to protect our citizens while doing more damage to our economy and our nation.

This lesson needs to be learned since the promotion of the Green New Deal is based on even worse science that totally ignores past historical climate changes and disruptions and is based on models that cannot even remotely take in consideration of natural events' role in climate changes and worse, ignores the positive benefit of carbon dioxide and its necessity in maintaining life on this planet.

The Green New Deal and the Failure of Climate Science

T he Left's Stalinist tactics were on full display when Attorney General Loretta Lynch confirmed in the summer of 2016, she was referring complaints to the Justice Department against oil companies for potential criminal prosecution. Sen. Sheldon Whitehouse of Rhode Island, a leading Democratic climate alarmist, had one goal: to jail oil company executives who disagree with his theories on how humans are destroying the planet. As Power Line's John Hinderaker noted, *"The Obama Administration's idea of a crime is not, apparently, violating federal laws and regulations and State Department procedures in a manner that exposes thousands of classified documents to our enemies. No, that is not the sort of conduct that is likely to draw an indictment from Loretta Lynch's Department of Justice. Obama's DOJ is more interested in trying to jail scientists who point out the rather obvious flaws in the government's desperate effort to convince Americans that global warming is our greatest threat."*[81]

The Obama administration and Democratic Senators were not just politicizing science, but they were *enforcing* their scientific worldview. They looked to the Justice Department and government bureaucracies to destroy fossil fuels companies and criminalize scientific difference. As John Hinderaker observed:

"The Soviets did that, in order to shore up the hopeless but government-favored theories of Lysenko. Until now, such conduct would have been unthinkable in an American administration. But Barack Obama, to his everlasting shame, is willing to emulate Josef Stalin by threatening criminal prosecution of those who disagree with the equally hopeless theories of Michael Mann et al. American history has come to an incredibly sad pass."[82]

While many viewed Donald Trump being a fascist, just remember which political party had used legal action against opponents, including using the IRS to go after conservative groups; having local Democrat prosecutors use Gestapo tactics to go after Scott Walker's supporters in Wisconsin, and now, threatening to use racketeering laws against climate realists who don't agree with the conventional wisdom that human activities is the key reason for climate change. So, who are the fascists, the Stalinists?

Meanwhile, the skeptics' worldview keeps being proven correct. I need to remind the reader that scientists whether they are skeptics or alarmist, believe *there is a general consensus that climate is changing, and no one denies climate is changing or the vast majority of scientists accept the overall climate is warming.* The real debate is *why* is it changing and whether a warmer planet will hurt or help humanity. The skeptic worldview notes the historical record that the climate has been changing since the planet was formed and there are skeptics who do not discount human involvement but contend that human activity is tempered by nature tempers it with the effects of nature and that human activity may not all that damaging. Some scientists are crediting the rise of carbon dioxide levels with enhancing plant life and aiding in increased agricultural output.

The alarmists view humans as the cause of modern-day climate change and don't even acknowledge or consider that natural events play a role. Nor can they explain how the planet is been getting greener over the past three decades as Dr. Pierre L. Gosselin, in reviewing the latest data noted, "This is not unexpected news to cool-headed climate realists. In August 2019, we reported on a German study showing how the globe had been greening for 3 decades. Based on satellite imagery, German *Wissenschaft* reported, "Vegetation on earth has been expanding for decades, satellite data show…Also not long ago a study by Venter et al (2018) found the Sahara desert had shrunk by 8% over the previous three decades. This is profound because the Sahara covers a vast area of some 9.2 million square kilometers. Eight percent means more than 700,000 square kilometers more area that's become green – an area almost as big as Germany and France combined."[83]

Science has yet to truly define what is causing present climate change or what the future will bring but it has not stopped the climate alarmists from predicting the end of the world scenario every five years or so and yet these predictions have yet to come to pass. Now John Kerry is telling us, and he added that he really means it this time, we have nine years before we reach the point of no return.

On February 19, 2021, for example, Kerry told "CBS This Morning," "The scientists told us three years ago that we had 12 years to avert the worst consequences of the climate crisis. We are now three years gone, so we have nine years left."

Several climate scientists contacted by *Washington Post* fact-checking columnist Glenn Kessler said that Kerry was misunderstanding statements made in a 2018 report by the Intergovernmental Panel on Climate Change (IPCC), whose gloomy forecasts about the future began with projections for 2030, which foresaw that the global temperature would rise by 1.5 degrees Celsius. Several climate scientists Kessler contacted said that Kerry overstated the harm near-term global temperature rises would cause, stating the ultimate goal was to stabilize planetary temperature by 2050.

"Please stop saying something globally bad is going to happen in 2030," said Oxford University climate scientist Myles Allen, a lead author of the IPCC report.: Bad stuff is already happening and every half a degree of warming matters, but the IPCC does not draw a 'planetary boundary' at 1.5 degrees C beyond which lie climate dragons.

"There's nothing magic about 1.5C," added Penn State climate scientist Michael E. Mann. There's no 'climate cliff' that we go off."

"2030 is not a magic date when future efforts to address climate change will no longer be effective," Kessler wrote. He awarded Kerry Two Pinocchio's for his misleading claim.[84]

The alarmists attempt to manipulate science was challenged in Donald Trump's administration, where climate skeptics and climate realists at least got the hearing they earned, but in Joe Biden's administration, it will be full speed ahead on alarmist science. The government scientists claim they proved the pause in climate temperature since 1998 didn't exist was deflated by another study that proved what climate realists have stated all along; we are in the midst of a pause in climate temperature change. From *Nature*, "*But in June last year, a study in* Science *claimed that the hiatus was just an artefact which vanishes when biases in temperature data are corrected...Now a prominent group of researchers is countering that claim, arguing in* Nature Climate Change *that even after correcting these biases the slowdown was real... "There is this mismatch between what the climate models are producing and what the observations are showing," says lead author John Fyfe, a climate modeler at the Canadian Centre for Climate Modeling and Analysis in Victoria, British Columbia. "We can't ignore it."*[85] Many of these researchers were considered climate alarmists and it showed that science is *not* settled which makes the efforts of Senator Whitehouse and others even more alarming since their own science is under siege.

The government is going after fossil fuel companies while the EPA is doing its best to destroy the coal industry and those high paying jobs for coal miners. Power Line's John Hinderaker wrote:

> "Actually, the oil companies have mostly been bystanders in the climate debate. But the Democrats are trying to deflect attention away from the fact that their global warming theory is crumbling in the face of the facts. The oil companies make convenient scapegoats.... What is outrageous about this is not the debate–no matter however flimsy, dishonest, and self-interested the government-funded alarmists may be–but rather the Democrats' attempt to shut the debate off by trying to imprison those who won't toe their line. This is the most blatant violation of the First Amendment that we have seen in a very long time."[86]

The Democratic Party, the so-called "party of science," has become the enemy of unfettered scientific research and free speech, as they are attempting to stop the free exchange of ideas and ensure that *their* ideas triumph. While much of the criticism in the article is valid, including Trump's own veiled threat against press freedom of speech, the *New York Times* has been missing in action when similar attacks by the left on political free speech and the tactics that have been used to silence Trump and others.

In California, there were legislators attempting to criminalize anyone who disagree with the notion that humans are the root cause of present climate change. Senate Bill 1161 or the California Climate Science Truth Accountability Act of 2016, would have allowed prosecutors to sue fossil fuel companies and think tanks who by their estimate, *"deceived or misled the public on the risk of climate change."*[87] The bill never made it out of committee and was not considered by the California Senate. This shows that many on the alarmists are preparing to criminalize any disagreement.

This is part of a broader effort to punish fossil fuels companies and think tanks to ensure uniformity of opinion on climate change and condemnation of anyone who disagrees with establishment opinions. It is as if the left ignores the First Amendment and cannot understand the scientific process where truth can be elusive and scientific advances pose more questions than answers. The left over the years has used the government, including the IRS, to attack conservative groups with the goal of intimidation and now ally themselves with big Tech oligarchies to keep ideas they don't like from reaching the public.

It has been recognized that we have seen a hiatus in temperature rise over the past two decades, but some climate alarmists' now use their usual cherry picking of data to prove the hiatus never happened and could be eliminated by looking at the data in a new way. The problem is that climate alarmists in Britain have stated that climate realists are right, the hiatus is real. So, the "settled science" is not really settled as alarmists cannot even agree on what is going on with their own computer models.

There have been a thousand studies over the past three years alone challenging the climate alarmists' worldview and showing that the science of climate change is far from being fully understood. This may explain why many alarmists and their allies in Congress and the media wants the debate shut down.

A report from *Insurance Journal* noted that dealing with global warming is over a $1.5 trillion a year global business. In 2011, money spent fighting global warming—consulting, renewables, green buildings, hybrid vehicles— increased 15% after a decade of solid growth. That does not include the billions of government research dollars directed to researchers, many of whom allied themselves with alarmists.

The companies owned by the Koch brothers have revenues that are a tenth of that spent on green technology. To keep those government contracts going, green technology companies have been major contributors to the Democratic Party. It is far from clear that these grants are helpful or do much more than subsidize activists.

Some climate scientists have called for federal funds to be cut off because the field is too ideological. Richard Lindzen, an emeritus professor at the Massachusetts Institute of Technology, noted, *"Even in 1990 no one at MIT called themselves a 'climate scientist,' and then all of a sudden everyone was. They only entered it because of the bucks; they realized it was a gravy train. You have to get it back to the people who only care about the science… They should probably cut the funding by 80 to 90 percent until the field cleans up, Climate science has been set back two generations, and they have destroyed its intellectual foundations."*[88]

Twenty scientists, led by Jagadish Shukla of George Mason University signed a petition to have the government prosecute "climate skeptics and deniers" with racketeering charges.[89] The message was clear: dissent when discussing climate change will not be tolerated. And as we saw with the government response to Covid-19 pandemic, bad science will lead to bad policies. The Green New Deal, with its goal of eliminating fossil fuels and nuclear energy will put billions on the brink of starvation. To understand what will happen if we enact the Green New Deal in its entirety, just look at Venezuela, an oil rich country that can't provide their people with food, clothing, and housing.

We can see just a tip of how the Green New Deal will change America, when President Biden rejoined the Paris accord. The Trump administration believed that we would lose 3 trillion dollars in GDP and 6.5 million jobs by joining this accord for a treaty that, at best, would reduce global temperatures by 0.17 degrees Celsius over the next century. Moreover, developing countries, along with India and China, would not be required to stop their own emissions until 2030. In the United States, we have dropped our own CO2 emissions by 14 percent since 2007 and that is the largest decline of any industrialized country without the need of a treaty. The reason is the increased use of natural gas, replacing coal. So, the economic and energy data will show that we don't need to radically change our economy to deal with climate change but instead allow the market to work and innovation to thrive. As for energy, nuclear energy would be a superior, non-polluting replacement for wind or solar to keep our manufacturing sector and economy going.

For the past half-century, the environmentalists have predicted doom and all of their predictions have failed to come anywhere close to happening. We have seen predictions of massive starvation due to overpopulation, reduction of resources just as oil and natural gas shortages, global cooling including a mini-ice age before we would fry to death in global warming. Institute for Energy Research Robert Bradley, Jr. observed, "Consider the career-long prognostications of John Holdren, Obama's two-term science advisor. "Some form of ecocatastrophe," he wrote (with Paul Ehrlich) in 1971, "seems almost certain to overtake us before the end of the [twentieth] century." In the mid-1980s, Holdren specifically predicted that as many as *one billion people* could die from climate change by 2020…Compared to Holdren's 128 deaths per 1,000 from climate change alone, *all* deaths last year were 7.6 per 1,000. Climate-related deaths, meanwhile, have dramatically declined due to increasing wealth and societal resiliency, a pillar of which is reliance on fossil fuels, which account for 84 percent of global energy usage today."[90]

Alarmists and their political allies often confuse weather with climate and never failed to hype any extreme weather events to prove the demise of humanity. As Robert Bradley added, "Global warming, which began in the mid-19th century with the end of the Little Ice Age, has been artfully magnified into something to be feared. Temperatures rise and fall at short time intervals, even within minutes. The (daily) diurnal cycle changes by tens of degrees, yet yearly global averages (very imperfectly estimated) change by hundredths of a degree."[91] David Simon, the son of Julian Simon, adds, "NASA's data set for global temperatures goes back to 1880 and shows that since that year, the earth's temperature has risen by only 1.14°C, an increase of 1.14°C over 139 years translates to an average increase of only 0.008°C per year." [92]

Much of these predictions are based on climate models that repeatedly overestimated recorded warming. This leads us to ask whether we should base public policy on unreliable models. As we have seen with the Covid-19 virus, models have proven useless and overestimated the death totals by a factor of least five times and turned a virus that had a infection fatality rate of .2 per 1000 into a modern-day bubonic plague. Just as the policies enacted to fight Covid-19 did more harm than the virus, so too will the policies of the Green New Deal do more harm than rising global temperatures.

The biggest threat to our prosperity is not climate change but the solutions designed to deal with the threat of climate change. While many climate alarmists predict starvation, famine and drought from unrestrained climate change, the reality is *that famine, drought, and starvation will come as result of their policies and not climate change.* Our biggest solution is innovation to continue our progress and be able to survive anything that nature serves up from floods, fires, hurricanes, and other natural disasters.

The biggest failure of the scientific class is refusal to engage in debate but instead censoring those ideas that challenges the conventional wisdom. As we have seen, many journals have refused to publish certain authors not due to the quality of their ideas or science but because they challenge the prevalent worldview. In the Covid-19 debate, the ideas of lockdowns advocated by Dr. Anthony Fauci and his allies has proven to be a disaster, and the thousands of scientists who have questioned the lockdown strategy and their cost have proven to be correct even as the media has censored much of their ideas. In the case of climate change, the alarmists have gone even farther by declaring their opponents not just skeptics or "deniers: but as criminals. 2020 was the year that pursuit of truth died.

Trump: For Better or Worse

Donald Trump was the enigma for many conservatives as we still wrestling with his legacy. His accomplishments were significant, and, in most eras, he would be viewed as a significant President. His economic plan lifted Americans incomes including those at the bottom, his Middle East policy managed to ally Sunni Arabs with Israel, and his recognition of China as a global adversary would have meant a shift in foreign policy if he won re-election. Then there was the Trump who refused to concede the election until January 6th, when the Capitol riot occurred. Trump's propensity for controversial statements and tweets antagonized many Americans and he certainly didn't always behave "presidentially."

In my book, *The Rise of National Populism and Democratic Socialism, What Our Response Should Be*, I compared Trump to Herbert Hoover, another businessman who became President. In 1929, Herbert Hoover became President. Before becoming President, Herbert Hoover's reputation was that of a self-made millionaire and brilliant manager. He served as Secretary of Commerce in the Harding and Coolidge Administrations and to many voters he was the Great Engineer who would bring his business expertise to government. While much of Hoover's reputation was that of a conservative, the reality was that Hoover was a progressive Republican. My father once reminded me that much of the New Deal began under Herbert Hoover and his run for

President in 1928 emphasized his business expertise and his managerial skills, which included his efforts in heading the American Relief Administration, which relieved the hunger of more than 200 million people In Europe from 1918 through 1922.

Hoover was a disciple of the Efficiency Movement, which sought to eliminate waste throughout the economy and society. This movement played an essential role in the Progressive era in the United States. The theory began that society and government would be better if experts fixed national problems once they were identified. Hoover felt comfortable with the Progressive movement. I bring Hoover up since Trump's campaign was like the Hoover appeal— a businessman who will run government by bringing in the best experts. *Trump doesn't talk about "reducing the size and role of government" but talks of managing the present government better.*

In her biography, *Herbert Hoover: Forgotten Progressive,* author Joan Hoff Wilson described Hoover's economic thinking:

> *The version of Hoover presented in the media's narrative of Hoover as champion of laissez faire bears little resemblance to the details of Hoover's life, the ideas he held, and the policies he adopted as president. Where the classical economists like Adam Smith had argued for uncontrolled competition between independent economic units guided only by the invisible hand of supply and demand, he talked about voluntary national economic planning arising from cooperation between business interests and the government . . .. Instead of negative government action in times of depression, he advocated the expansion of public works, avoidance of wage cuts,*

increased rather than decreased production—mea-
sures that would expand rather than contract pur-
chasing power." [93]

St. Lawrence University economist Steve Horwitz added, *"Hoover was also a long-time critic of international free trade, and favored increased inheritance taxes, public dams, and, significantly, government regulation of the stock market. This was not the program of a devotee of laissez faire, and he was determined to use the Commerce Department to implement it."* [94] Trump, like Hoover, opposes international free trade and in the past talked of surtaxes on the rich. The similarity between the progressive Hoover and the progressive Trump were eerie to many of us in 2015 and through the 2016 primary.

I theorize that Trump's model of Republicanism would be like Hoover's and Richard Nixon's. Nixon was a statist as president, including creating new bureaucracies like the Occupational Health and Safety Administration and the Environmental Protection Agency as well as wage and price controls. Nixon's goal was to make government work for the Middle Class and his supporters – his silent majority. However, Trump broke more toward Reagan on domestic policy, except for his trade policies, which closely resembled the GOP of the 1920's. Trump's goal was to make government work for the middle class, those who were left behind over the past two decades. Trump's policies benefitted minorities and those at the bottom as those at the bottom and minorities saw their income go up until the pandemic. The pandemic sent much of the middle class, lower class, and minorities income lower and for wiping out the gains many made during Trump's first three years as president.

Richard Nixon's own economic policies, along with the paralysis of the Watergate scandal, led to the recession of 1973-75 and to the stagflation of the 1970's, which included slow or no growth along with high inflation at the end of the decade under Jimmy Carter. It wasn't until the Reagan years that the back of inflation was broken. After, we saw more than two decades of economic growth resulting in a rise of income for the middle class that continued during the Clinton administration, but it was the supply side economics of Reagan that shook America out of lethargy. Reagan faced a different challenge, raging inflation and high marginal tax rates that was sucking many in the middle class into higher tax brackets. Today, the marginal tax rates are considerably lower to go with recent Trump reductions of corporate taxes. Even the highest Biden corporate tax rates will still be lower than what they were before Trump lowered the rate. (Biden's corporate tax rates would place the United States near the highest in the developed world.)

While many Trump supporters tried to compare their guy to Reagan[95] throughout the 2016 election, there are significant differences. Unlike Trump and Hoover, Reagan was an accomplished politician who had been on the political scene for decades and had already run for president once. Before that, he was a well- known actor and even as an actor, he had a keen interest in politics. Before Reagan became president, he had been fighting for conservative ideals for three decades and understood the political process as well as the ideas behind them. Kiron Skinner, Annelise Skinner and the late Martin Anderson's own research confirmed his substantive knowledge of the issues by reviewing and publishing many of his diaries and other private writings.

In 1967, Reagan was invited to be part of a debate with Robert F Kennedy on American foreign policy and destroyed him and eleven years later, many felt he won a debate with Bill Buckley on whether the U.S. should withdraw from the Panama Canal Zone. These two debates showed he had the ability to go toe to toe with some of the best debaters of his era.

There is one similarity between Ronald Reagan and Donald Trump is that both were consistently underrated. Trump in 2016 as a debater succeeded with his attitude, not on what he knew. The four words, "Make America Great Again," exhibits Trump's mindset. He wanted to reverse the decline he saw. Trump may prove to be more of an experimenter than following a set game plan, seeking what works. Another similarity with Reagan and Trump is that both reached blue-collar workers. In 1980, these voters were called Reagan Democrats. Now they are called Trump Republicans.

How often have we heard what a great dealmaker Trump is? How many people will remember that Reagan was a master of negotiations? When Trump during the election made the case that Reagan worked with Tip O' Neill, he did not remember Reagan did not deal with Tip O' Neill, *he dealt against O'Neill* by working with moderate Democrats to get much of his budget and tax policies passed. Reagan had a Democratic majority in the House plus heavy opposition in the Republican-controlled Senate. Many moderate Republicans were against his economic plans and he did not deal with O'Neill. Instead, he dealt with many of the moderate and conservative Democrats and went around O'Neill.

Reagan's deal making with the Russians was exemplary, but Reagan's success is that he dealt from strength. The nuclear freeze was in full force during his first administration as the left were trying to undermine his military buildup by keeping America from putting Pershing missiles into Europe to counter the Soviet SS-20. Reagan's first goal was to rebuild the military before dealing with the Russians and to wait for the right moment to call for arms reductions on both sides. That moment did not come until Mikhail Gorbachev took over the Soviet empire in 1985. During his second term., Reagan successfully negotiated the removal of intermediate-range nuclear missiles in both Europe and Russia in

1987 because the year before, he walked out of the Reykjavik conference on nuclear arms reduction. Reagan's policy set the stage for the collapse of the Soviet Union in 1991.

Reagan walked into the White House with a worldview and a plan to go with that worldview. Unlike Reagan, Trump did not have a history of consistent ideology when he entered the White House and he supported Economic nationalism and consistent supporters of protectionism. This was shown in his cabinet appointments, as he selected conservatives such as Rick Perry and Scott Pruitt but others just as Steve Mnunchin were outsiders. Trump appointments come from all factions of the Republican Party and in the case of Mnunchin, a political novice with no public record as a political activist other than his donations, mostly to Democrats. Trump's ideology was originally based on Trump's personal brand, divorced from a consistent worldview. While Reagan began his career as a Democrat, his move to the right aligned with his movement toward traditional Republican values. Trump did show that he belonged to the right as his court appointments, tax and regulation policies showed. His foreign policy was the more modest approach that George W. Bush ran on in 2000 before 9/11. His view of "America First" was not isolationism as much as ensuring that American interests came first and that included an energy plan that allowed America through fracking to challenge OPEC as the leading producers of oil natural gas and oil and having our allies pay their fair share of their own defense.

Throughout the 2016 election, Trump's two signature issues were immigration and trade. He exploited the yawning gap between the views of the elites in both parties and the public on these issues. He feasted on the public discontent over a government that can't be bothered to enforce its own laws on immigration no matter how many times it says it will. With the Biden Administration's first steps in reversing border security of Trump years, this only reinforced the political class willingness to obliterate our borders and open the tap of illegal immigrants coming into the country.

Nixon ran in 1968 on behalf of the silent majority who were overtaxed, whose sons were fighting in Vietnam and who witnessed crime going up. Nixon ran a law-and-order campaign and when he governed, he expanded the welfare state in his first term while giving us the Environmental Protection Agency. His goal was to rein in the bureaucratic state and create a conservative big government that worked for the middle class. He did not reduce government spending or the power of the administrative state.

Like Nixon, Trump ran on a law-and-order platform, including standing up for a new generation of forgotten Americans, many of whom fought in Afghanistan and Iraq. And as 2020 showed, the left's attempt to defund the police and cut budgets across the country only increased crime, much of it in urban centers.

Trump in his own way succeeded in doing what others claim conservatives needed to do. He significantly increased GOP vote totals among minorities. Only George W, Bush and Ronald Reagan outperformed Trump's vote totals among Hispanics in 2020 and Trump's Black votes percentages were higher than both men and only Richard Nixon and Gerald Ford exceeded Trump percentages with blacks. While exit polls had Trump at 12 percent among Blacks, one post-election poll had Trump support among Blacks at 18%. At least 1,500,000 more Blacks and Hispanics voted for Trump in 2020 than 2016.

Trump's failure was his inability to get to over 50% plus and after two election cycles, his coalition was stuck at 47%. One factor that hurt Trump was the collapsed of Third Parties with Libertarians going from 3.5% to 1 %. He increased his numbers among minorities and that in previous elections would have been enough to secure victory, but he lost ground among college educated whites, in particular college educated men. The question remains is how much of that was due to their disdain for his personality and how much was due to his policies.

Trump's influence on the party is significant for he built a new coalition of attracting many poorer and blue-collar whites to the Republican flag and his game plan for developing support among minorities is showing fruit. Trump did what we at Americas PAC have suggested, build a coalition around rural and blue-collar whites while adding significant numbers of minorities. His biggest failure was suburban America in 2020. In 2016, Trump had a four percent lead in the suburbs but in 2020, he lost the suburban vote by two percent, a six-point swing. The coalition is within reach of a Republican victory, but it entails finding a politician who can woo the suburban vote while keeping Trump Republicans loyal to the G.O.P. and make further inroads among minorities.

Among those who might be that candidate in 2024 could be Ron DeSantis who has shown his ability to guide his state through the pandemic while maintaining Florida's economic performance. In January 2021, Florida had lower unemployment among the larger states, with death totals from the Covid-19 virus lower than most of the larger Democratic States.

unemployment

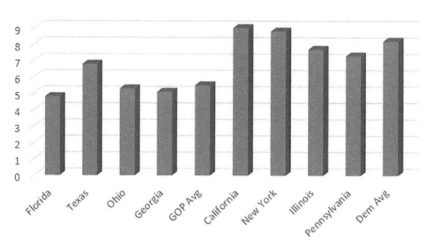

Top 8 Death per capital

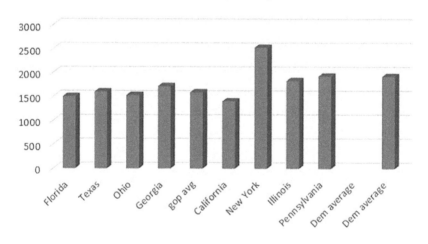

As for Trump, I don't believe that he will run again, and his legal troubles will still be with him. The battle to see Trump punished will continue a state level and New York City and Biden's Justice Department will certainly carry on their own jihad against Trump and his family. There is a precedence for this as Franklin Roosevelt pursued members of the Hoover administration—and. in particular Andrew Mellon— legally and modern-day Democratic Party is even more nasty, and Joe Biden will not lose sleep over his DOJ or some state attorney general pursuing the Trump family until they find something to jail him or members of his family or bankrupt them. For many Democrats, Trump was an affront to them, and it is their attention to wipe out any aspect of Trumpism. Trump's influence may be as a kingmaker in the foreseeable future and talk of Trump starting his own cable? network or social media platform will be stop this effort to affect the direction of the Republican Party.

Trumpism is part of the conservative movement, and the GOP and conservatives need to understand that for their own future success and for the sake of the country, a synergy between Trump populism and conservatism is not only within reach but also a necessity.

There is no place for a "never-Trumper" movement within the conservative coalition directed at his supporters but an acceptance that they are integral part of the coalition without which the GOP and conservative's movement can survive. The never Trumper movement should have ended in 2016 after the primary for obvious reasons, —the Democrats were far worse. Biden Administration has already proven along with much of the leadership class that they intend to institute a socialist regime that threatens the very fabric of our society. Trump may have his weaknesses, but he was preferable to Joe Biden and the rest of the Democratic Party. As I detailed in my previous book, *The Rise of National Populism and Democratic Socialism*, the Democratic Party is now the socialist party of America. : But the fundamental question remains: what about the GOP and the conservative movement?. Where do we go from here?

Trumpism Without Trump: The Synergy of Trump Populism and Conservatism

In 2014, before the "Trump coalition" was formed, we campaigned in Illinois. Republicans made a strong showing when they took the governor's seat, and two congressional seats and Senator Dick Durbin was held to 53% of the vote against weak competition. Throughout the campaign, we ran ads that argued that rising government spending and debt reduced voters' economic opportunities, and these ads succeeded in persuading voters to vote for Republicans. Voters, our customers, knew that the Obama economic plan produced eight years of stagnation and that they no longer benefitted from Democratic policies. In 2016, the rise of Donald Trump showed that many Republicans didn't even trust their own party to follow through on producing opportunities to succeed. So, they nominated an outsider.

For years, Democrats have been good at framing their ideas as a way to solve their customer's problems but the customers, namely voters, are no longer automatically buying the Democratic plan and for the most part, their campaign in 2020 was about "Hate Donald Trump" and not talk much about their socialist game plan. But now they are governing, they must present their agenda.

As I mentioned in my previous book, the GOP has yet to decide on what kind of party they will be and what they will emphasize. Trump was solid on taxes and regulations; his foreign policy was a return to the more modest approach that George W. Bush campaigned on in 2000. But Trump increased government debt and government spending. Trump's spending plans looked modest compared to what Democrats have pushed for the past four years and are now proposing. What he promised to do was to "Make America Great Again." As Americas Majority Foundation associate JD Johannes noted, "Too often politicians and their consultants view voters as blocs or market segments. *For Democrats, this makes sense since they view voters as part of demographic groups, but Republicans and conservatives succeed when they view voters not as blocs with specific issues but address major macro concerns."*

The pandemic produced a fissure within the country and many in the middle class saw their incomes decline. Michael Lind observed, "Some on the populist right and anti-capitalist left interpret the prolonged state lockdowns as conspiracy by big business against small business. It is easy to see how people could reach this conclusion. Many small firms had been destroyed during the pandemic by government-mandated bans and social distancing rules while bigger firms had an easier time. According to Inequality. org, between Mid-March 2020 and February 2021, the wealth of U.S. billionaires grew by 1.3 trillion. But the wealth gains for the rich have gains for the rich have come mostly from their disproportionate representation in stock market, not from the ability to steal customers from small companies that have gone under." [96] Regardless of the cause, the cost of the pandemic had unequal consequences for a good portion of the Republican coalition.

Voters noticed that while they got money from the stimulus to tie them over from a government induced plan to stop the economy cold, the ability to start up their lives proved difficult and for many as they entered 2021, the Federal government and many state governments did not want to give up their control while many governors, mostly in red states, decided to open the economy. (The latter opening was opposed by much of the political class located in Washington DC and the scientific class.)

We noticed this in a report a few years back, following the 2012 elections, "The Republican Party does not have a problem attracting women voters. It has a problem attracting *minority voters*, both male and female. The aggregate of 9,000 plus interviews with registered voters in 2012 Gallup's tracking poll shows that 50% of white women favor Romney with only 41% preferring Obama. In final 2012 exit polls, this margin increased to 12% as Romney carried 56% of white women to Obama's 44%. Married poll respondents favor Romney over Obama 54%—39%. If you are looking at a married, white woman, you were likely looking at a Romney vote. Obama's electoral advantage in women was with unmarried, minority women. Conservative strategists looking to mitigate Obama's lead among women should focus on minority women who are struggling under the failure of Democratic economic policies. This data was similar in 2020 as White women went for Trump 55% to 44% which was a two percent increase from 2016 but Black women went for Biden by a 90% to 9% and Black Women were half as likely to vote for Trump as Black men. Hispanics women voted for Biden 69% to 30% compared to Hispanics men who voted for Biden by a 59% to 36%. Minority women were significantly more Democratic than White women and even minority men. In the case of Black voters, twice as many Black women voted than Black men and Hispanic women made up 62% of Hispanic voters. White men made of 35% of the vote versus 32% of White women, so minority women make up a lion's share of minority voters." [97]

Married women voted for Trump, but single women voted for Biden. Married status does point to party affiliations and one explanation is that most single females make less than their married counterparts, and many minorities single females also have children and live-in poverty or close to the poverty line.

Thirty-five percent of black families headed by single parents live in poverty compared to 7% of married black families, and 38% of Hispanic single female head of household hold live in poverty compared to 12% of married Hispanic couples. Living in a single-parent home increases the chances of children living in poverty and receiving government assistance, leaving them more likely to support big government programs and income transfers. But those programs have done nothing to help women and children rise out of poverty.

Marriage is a significant factor in poverty and as Heritage Foundation senior fellow Robert Rector noted, "Marriage remains America's strongest anti-poverty weapon. As husbands disappear from the home, poverty, and welfare dependence will increase. Children and parents will suffer as a result."[98] Family structure plays a factor in combating poverty and the evidence shows a decline in family formation plays a role in the number of minorities in poverty.

Education is a factor in whether a woman will have a child out of wedlock but regardless of education, married women are less likely to live in poverty than single parents. Only 15% of women who are married and without a high school diploma live in poverty, whereas 47% of single female head of household dropouts live in poverty. Thirty-one percent of single female head of households with a high school diploma live in poverty compared to only 5% of married families, and 24% of single female head of households with a college degree lives in poverty while only 3.2% of married women with a college degree live in poverty. Nearly 9% of single women with a bachelor's degree or higher live-in poverty compared to 1.5% of married families where couples have a bachelor's degree or higher. Something has obviously gone horribly wrong with family formation; and the hardest hit are minority women and children.

"*The gag rule about marriage is nothing new,*" Rector writes in his Heritage Foundation report. "*At the beginning of the War on Poverty, a young Daniel Patrick Moynihan (later Ambassador to the United Nations and Senator from New York), serving in the Administration of President Lyndon Johnson, wrote a seminal report on the negative effects of declining marriage among blacks. The Left exploded, excoriating Moynihan and insisting that the erosion of marriage was either unimportant or benign. Four decades later, Moynihan's predictions have been vindicated. The erosion of marriage has spread to whites and Hispanics with devastating results. But the taboo on discussing the link between poverty and the disappearance of husbands remains as firm as it was four decades ago.*"[99]

Marriage is the key to eliminating poverty because it causes husbands to earn more to care for their family. As Manhattan Institute fellow Kay S. Hymowitz pointed out, "Marriage itself, it seems, encourages male productivity. One study by Donna Ginther and Madeline Zavodny examined men who'd had "shotgun" marriages and thus probably hadn't been planning to tie the knot. The shotgun husbands nevertheless earned more than their single peers did." [100]

As long as couples decline to marry, the ability of policymakers to institute policies to raise minority families out of poverty have limits. What is clear from the past 50 years is that the path away from poverty is not more government assistance, but jobs, economic growth and encouraging two-parent families.

The question that remains is how much is being a single female voting Democratic dependent upon being a minority. The conservative campaign strategy of benign neglect toward minority voters is a significant source of the "women gap" for Republican candidates. Romney, after all, led Obama in 2012 among white women and Trump continued this in 2016 and 2020. Minority women are a significant factor in the Democratic lead among women in general and single women. The key element here is what policies would be effective to persuade women, in particular minority women? Being married is an important factor in escaping poverty and moving up the economic ladder so what policies would encourage marriage over the long haul and what policies would benefit minority women? Ron DeSantis received 18% of black women's votes in Florida in 2018 and one reason was his support for school choice.

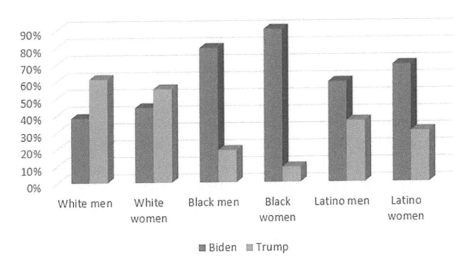

women voters

Biden   Trump

Except for bailed out bankers and recipients of green technology loan guarantees, every economic sector and demographic group were hit hard by the Great Recession of 2007-2009. One demographic group that suffered the most were young people aged

18-29, with young African Americans and Hispanics the hardest hit. They directly felt the brunt of the Obama Administration's failed economic policies, and many are feeling the brunt of the pandemic lockdowns.

Youth voters

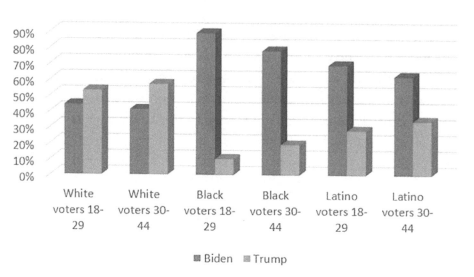

Republicans need to find a new generation of voters who will embrace the GOP's job creating economic policies. Understanding this potential new group of voters and how to reach them requires a close look at their underlying demographics, because young voters are rapidly becoming minority voters.

"*The surge in the minority vote we saw in 2008* **was** *the surge in the youth vote,*" Sean Trende writes in his book *The Lost Majority.* [101]

Trende observed that Obama's lead among all voters, including the 18-24 age cohort, was less pronounced once non-white voters were taken out of the calculation. "*These groups swung toward Obama largely because these segments of the electorate became much more heavily minority in 2008, as the country continued to* "brown "demographically and as Obama turned out minority voters in droves...It does suggest GOP does not have a minority problem and youth problem. It is the same problem." [102]The younger a voter is, the more likely the voter is an ethnic or racial minority. Only 57% of Americans between 18 and 29 are white. Attracting young voters and minority voters should be seen as a unified effort for national Republican campaigns and in states like California, Texas, Florida, and Illinois.

The Democrats continues to count on an upsurge in minority voters as well as youth voters. In 2008, Obama garnered 66% of the youth vote, which is the first time that either party had more than 60% among young voters 18-29. When minorities are taken out of the mix of young voters, Obama's margin among the young was not much different that the general election results of 54% to 46%. Among 18–29-year-old voters in 2008, Hispanics voted for Obama 76-19 and African Americans voted for Obama 96-4. Hispanic youth voted more for Obama than other Hispanic age groups.

In 2020, Biden cornered 56% of the voters under 45, many of whom were part of the 66% who voted for Obama in 2008. It appears that Republicans have made some inroads of younger voters as they are getting a higher percentage of the young than they did 12 years ago but they are still running significantly behind the Democrats and as with women, it is minorities that make the difference. Republicans with younger voters and women is more a reflection of Republicans problems with minorities than their problems with younger voters and women.

18 to 44

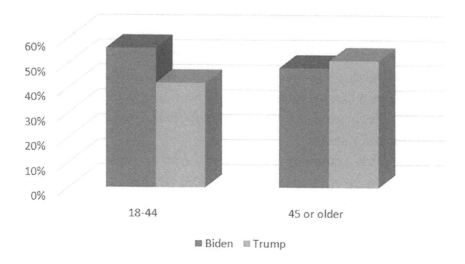

18-44   45 or older

■ Biden   ■ Trump

Just as with women, Trump won the white youth vote, winning the 18-29 years old vote 53-44 and capturing the 30–44-year-old 57% to 41%. The Republican margin for white 30-44 years old is close to Trump's vote total of 58% of overall White voters. Ten percent of Black voters between 18 and 29 voted for Trump and 19% of those between 30-44 voted for Trump. Blacks 30 to 44 years proved more likely to vote for Trump than any other group and Blacks between the age 18 to 44 are more likely to vote for Trump that Blacks 45 years old and older. Twenty-eight percent of Hispanics 18 to 29 and 34% of Hispanics 30 to 44 voted for Trump. It should be noted that Blacks aged 18-44 make up 50% of Black voting totals and Hispanics 18 to 44 make up 62% of the Hispanic voting population. While Hispanics 60 and older gave Trump 40% of their vote, they make up only 15% of Hispanic voters whereas Blacks 60 and over make up 25% of Black voters and white voters over age 60 make up 38% of the total vote. Two out of every three white voters are over age 45r. White voters ages 18 to 44 make up only 33% of the white voting population, while 50% of black voters are between 18-44 and 62% of Hispanics voters are 18-44. Younger minority voters make up a more significant percentage of their voting bloc than white voters do and minorities have a higher percentage of voters 18-44 than America as a whole has. Republicans and conservatives need to understand that minority voters will make up a larger share of the voting population over the next three decades.

Youth voters

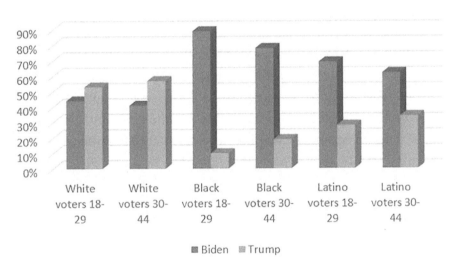

In the 2016 general election, Sen. Marco Rubio in his Senate race not only outperformed Trump in Florida, but Rubio overall did better among minorities. He showed that reformist conservatism could be sold beyond the Republican base as he received 17% of black voters statewide and 48% of Hispanic voters. Rubio received 62% of the Cuban voters and nearly 40% of non-Cuban voters, which made up nearly 63% of Republican Hispanic voters in Florida. While Trump received slightly more white voters (64 percent) compared to Rubio with 62 percent in his Senate re-election bid, Trump received about half as many votes as Rubio did among Black voters and only received 35% as many Hispanic votes as Rubio did. While Trump received 54% of Cuban Hispanic voters, he received only 26% of non-Cuban Hispanic voters, about three percent less than he received from Hispanic voters nationally.

Reform conservatism can be sold to many Democrats, including minorities. The debate on taxes and immigration showed while there were differences in approaches between Cruz and Rubio's beliefs, both senators had the same objective of expanding conservatism to include blue-collar whites and minorities. It could be argued that Rubio is not much different in his tactics in appealing to voters as Trump. In Florida, Rubio's tactics ensured an election victory in 2016 and Trump won Florida by a close margin.

In 2020, Trump won 56% of Cuban voters in Florida and won 31% of Puerto Rican voters, and while Trump won a slightly higher percentage of Black voters in Florida than he did in 2016, it was still below the national average and below what Rubio won in 2016. Trump won Florida by a larger margin than he did in 2016.

Ron DeSantis's performance in the 2018 Florida governor's race is worth looking at, since he is a leading candidate for the 2024 Republican nomination provided, he wins re-election as governor in 2022. Overall, DeSantis won 44% of Hispanic voters and 14% of Black voters but he won 18% of Black women voters, much of it due to his support for school choice. Ron DeSantis won more Hispanic voters than Trump did two years previously, but a little bit less than what Trump won in 2020.

Trump in 2020 managed 55% of suburban voters in Florida compared to 53% for Ron DeSantis in 2018, but he won only 61% of rural voters compared to 69% for DeSantis. DeSantis won 42% of the urban voters and Trump won 44% of urban areas. Ron DeSantis won a squeaker of an election in 2018, but there is evidence he could put together a Trumpian coalition of rural and blue-collar voters and could even add more minority voters.

DeSantis's ability to attract minorities proved decisive in winning the 2018 election. His ability to weather the Wuhan virus storm and keep his state economically vibrant helps him, while Florida's death totals from the pandemic were better than many other comparable large states. By January 2021, Florida's unemployment dropped below 5%, the lowest of the eight most populous states and deaths per capita were lower than all those eight large states except California. (If one adjusts for Florida's having proportionately older voters than California, the differences between the two states in pandemic death rates disappeared.)

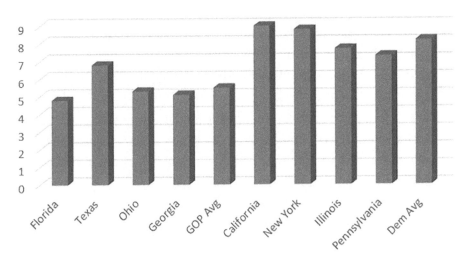

unemployment January data

Top 8 Death per capita

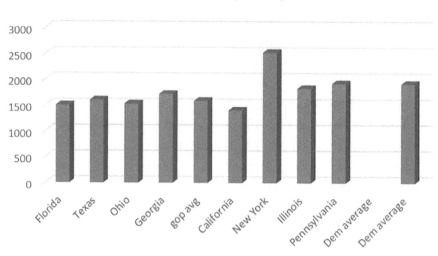

DeSantis showed his mastery of a serious crisis, managing to keep his state's economy afloat while outperforming Democrat governors Andrew Cuomo and Gavin Newsom throughout the pandemic. DeSantis's goal of returning Florida to normal succeeded because he understood the virus and how best to deal with its aftermath by first concentrating on protecting the most vulnerable. His ability to vaccinate his citizens quickly compared favorably to many of his governor counterparts.

DeSantis combined competence with a drive and vision of how to tame the virus and get people back to work and children back to school. While many governors chose control and economic restrictions, DeSantis moved toward a freer economy. The one lesson for Republicans and conservatives that DeSantis teaches is not to depend upon the experts. DeSantis realized quickly that Dr. Anthony Fauci and others overestimated the lethality of the virus and underestimated the economic devastation of the lockdown. Others like Dr. Scott Atlas, Dr. John Ioannidis, Dr. Jay Bhattacharya, and Martin Kulldorff felt the lockdowns beyond the initial fifteen days in March and April 2020 would produce more deaths over the long term and damage the fabric of society. The price of lock-down would be too high, they contended, and DeSantis joined the lockdown skeptics. As it turned out, much of the criticism the lockdown skeptics made early in the pandemic proved valid and DeSantis demonstrated that the strategy they recommended was more effective than the punitive lockdown strategy. *He also showed the politicization of the scientific class and the need to go beyond them to get better science to base policy on.*

Andrew Cuomo, lauded throughout 2020 as the gold standard by the compliant media, found that for all his bluster and media good will, his record spoke for itself. He had more deaths and a floundering economy. As 2021 dawned, Cuomo's record showed that 1000 per million more died of Covid and at a cost of nearly 30,000 per million more unemployed compared to Florida. New York City itself was damaged even worse and there was a mass exodus from the city, with many New York City residents heading for Florida. For Republicans, DeSantis showed that when given advice from experts, verify what they are saying is actually true and the policy recommendations they propose will not prove disas-trous. The second lesson DeSantis provides is that. if the leadership class is wrong on an issue, challenge their advice and do not give in. DeSantis's success in the pandemic like other Republican gover-nors, including Kristi Noem, points the way for a new Republican Party that will combine conservative and free market principles and anchor those free market conservative principles to the new populism to build upon the Trump coalition.

The original key to winning 2016 was for Republicans and con-servatives to create an alliance that combines the concerns of dif-ferent groups, including those who are concerned for gun rights, privacy rights, and those who fear the loss of religious freedom, in stopping expanding government while increasing economic freedom and economic opportunity. This coalition appeared threatened by Donald Trump's national populism but as the 2016 election proceeded, Trump adopted many of the Republican Party's ideas about reforming government spending and tax policies that promoted growth and opportunity. The Republican candidates who articulated a message of ***A Fair Opportunity to Succeed*** put themselves in the best position to win whether nationally, state-wide, or in Congressional districts.

Going beyond 2021, the message should still be the same: *a fair opportunity to succeed.* What voters want to see are solutions to their problems, beginning with stagnant income. However, past solutions may no longer be applicable today as many voters are not as affected by drops in marginal tax rates, but they are affected by a shrinking private sector compared to an ever expanding federal and state? government.

JD Johannes added, *"People have been hearing about tax cuts for a generation and it is not a motivating factor for most voters. I doubt voters see tax cuts as the solution to their problems. And in our current situation, more free capital sloshing around is not a guarantee of innovation that will drive value creation, higher wages and more jobs. Tax cuts are not bad...the voters just don't see them delivering what they want...Factories run on electricity and the US is in a position to have the cheapest, most reliable electricity in the world. Regulations that increase the cost of energy reduce our competitive position in manufacturing."* Supply-siders must realize that an economic recovery is not just about lowering taxes but removing those forces that inhibit economic growth, thus giving an American worker chance at advancement.

It is time to realize that government spending is an important consideration of a prosperous society, and prosperity won't last long with massive government deficits or long-term federal debt that is nearly equal to the overall productive value of the nation. As America slipped in the Heritage Foundation ratings of economic liberty over the past fifteen years from being free to almost free, it is no coincidence that the average American had stagnant income growth and the nation had slow economic growth compared to other past recoveries. (In fairness, the decline in economic growth began during the George W. Bush administration and accelerated during the Obama years.)

Many argue that while Americans don't view increased government spending as a solution to their problems, they are not keen on seeing their favorite programs cut.

Imagine if a president simply stated, "We will keep the budget the same for the next four years." There is a recent model to this as the Republicans called Obama's bluff in putting a sequester in place starting in 2011. The most significant budget deficit reduction during the Obama years occurred after the sequester was passed and while this did result in cuts in the Defense Department budget, a spending freeze doesn't mean you can't set priorities. One way to begin the process of spending reduction is simply review the different departments and ask about each one, "Can we live without it?" One place to start is the Department of Energy, which the fracking revolution has made obsolete. If you eliminate departments, you eliminate the need to spend in a particular area and you can send government funds to areas where the needs are greater.

In 2010, President Obama's own budget commission recommended a combination of budget cutting, tax reforms including lower marginal tax rates and closing loopholes. So in 2010, there were Democrats willing to listen to reasonable ideas about the budget and there were bipartisan solutions that could gain traction. (The commission's overall tax plans would have increased taxes on most Americans, but the commission accepted the need to lower marginal tax rates as well as the need to increase overall wealth. The commission also supported other tax reform plans that were revenue neutral.)

Regulation is another area to discover the supply side, and this is one area that Trump has gotten right with his plan to eliminate older regulations when new ones are created. The regulations imposed by Dodd-Frank have benefited the bigger banks and financial institutions since they have the capital to deal with the increased regulations compared to smaller and medium size banks. Since Dodd-Frank, bigger banks have gained market share at the expense of smaller ones, the very banks that serve much of Main Street. This simply shows that regulations do hurt the middle class and the institutions they depend upon. The EPA's war on coal has made it more difficult for coal to compete with natural gas and has cost the coal industry many high paying jobs. So, supply siders need to concentrate not just on reducing taxes but understanding that reducing spending and regulations will also have the supply side effect of increasing growth.

The Achilles heel of Democratic economic policies is that they are so concerned with what individuals make or don't make that they forget that a growing private sector provides opportunity for all. As John F. Kennedy remarked a half-century ago, "A rising tide lifts all boats."

The Democratic War on Freedom

While many view Donald Trump being a fascist, just remember which political party had used legal action against opponents, including using the IRS to go after conservative groups; having local Democrat prosecutors use Gestapo tactics to go after Scott Walker's supporters in Wisconsin, and threatened to use racketeering laws against climate realists who didn't agree with the conventional wisdom that human activities is the primary reason for climate change.

What we saw over the past year with riots caused by Antifa and BLM was not the first that the left used violence. This has been going on for past seven years, including the riots in Ferguson, Missouri in 2014 and the riots that devastated Baltimore in 2015. In 2016, the left conducted riots aimed at Donald Trump rallies, where their goal was to stop Trump from speaking and to intimidate his supporters with the threat of violence. The rioters' view was since Trump was a fascist, it was okay to break the law and threaten his supporters. The left stifled free speech whether it is keeping conservative speakers from speaking at college campuses, including threatening violence, using the IRS to target conservative groups during the Obama/Biden administration, using goon squads to intimidate Republican candidate supporters, or threatening those they disagree with jail time.

The left's interference with Trump rallies during the 2016 primary season resulted in violence in San Jose. After the San Jose riot, the Democratic mayor failed to blame the rioters, but instead blamed the Trump campaign. Nor was this the first violence at a Trump rally. A week earlier, 18 people were injured and 35 people arrested at a San Diego rally. In another violent incident in Costa Mesa, California, two months before that, crowds smashed the windows of a police car and tried to flip it over. During the Illinois primary, hooligans shut down a Trump rally.

In Wisconsin, the left's efforts to silence the right resulted in a partisan witch-hunt against supporters of Republican Gov. Scott Walker. While supposedly enforcing campaign regulations, Milwaukee County Democratic prosecutor John Chisholm used campaign finance laws in a cynical war against conservative organizations in the state. Local law enforcement shined floodlights in their victims' front yards, and armed officers seized documents, computers, cell phones and other devices from activists' homes.

Chisholm was conducting a "John Doe investigation" and which the targets of the investigation were barred from talking about it. Eric O' Keefe, director of the Wisconsin Club for Growth, violated the gag order and openly spoke out against the war waged against him by the Democrats and decided he would stand in his way of the Democratic manipulation of Wisconsin campaign laws. Judge Rudolph Randa, hearing O' Keefe's horror stories, halted the Democratic corruption. In 2015, the Wisconsin Supreme Court ruled that Chisholm had no case and O'Keefe and other conservatives were innocent.

Just read how Judge Rudolph Randa described the "John Doe investigation", *"Early in the morning of October 3, 2013, armed officers raided the homes of R.J. Johnson, WCFG (Wisconsin Club for*

Growth) advisor Deborah Jordahl, and several other targets across the state. ECF No. 5-15, O 'Keefe Declaration, ¶ 46. Sheriff Deputy Vehicles used bright floodlights to illuminate the targets' homes. Deputies executed the search warrants, seizing business papers, computer equipment, phones, and other devices, while their targets were restrained under police supervision and denied the ability to contact their attorneys. Among the materials seized were many of the Club 's records that were in the possession of Ms. Jordahl and Mr. Johnson. The warrants indicate that they were executed at the request of GAB investigator Dean Nickel.

On the same day, the Club 's accountants and directors, including O 'Keefe, received subpoenas demanding that they turn over more or less all of the Club 's records from March 1, 2009 to the present. The subpoenas indicated that their recipients were subject to a Secrecy Order, and that their contents and existence could not be disclosed other than to counsel, under penalty of perjury. The subpoenas' list of advocacy groups indicates that all or nearly all right-of-center groups and individuals in Wisconsin who engaged in issue advocacy from 2010 to the present are targets of the investigation...The defendants are pursuing criminal charges through a secret John Doe investigation against the plaintiffs for exercising issue advocacy speech rights that on their face are not subject to the regulations or statutes the defendants seek to enforce. This legitimate exercise of O 'Keefe 's rights as an individual, and WCFG 's rights as a 501(c)(4) corporation, to speak on the issues has been characterized by the defendants as political activity covered by Chapter 11 of the Wisconsin Statutes, rendering the plaintiffs a subcommittee of the Friends of Scott Walker and requiring that money spent on such speech be reported as an in-kind campaign contribution. This interpretation is simply wrong.” [103]

This was a blatant attempt by Democrats to shut down conservative organizations in Wisconsin and was a precursor for the left's war against conservatives. What we saw with the censorship we are witnessed with Big Tech during the 2020 elections began in the Obama/Biden administration. We can expect similar attempts by the left to use the state to fight conservatives in the future.

Violence as Leftist Tactics

The summer of violence in 2020 began a battle that culminated in the attack on the Capitol on January 6th, 2021, which was the only major riot started by the right. The Left, including members of Black Lives Matter (BLM) and Antifa, committed almost all political violence in the U.S. in 2020. Billions of dollars of property were destroyed and as many as 30 people died, including former St. Louis police chief David Dorn, murdered by thugs who filmed his death.

Andy Ngo has been one of the few journalists who has penetrated Antifa and discovered a terrorist group protected by much of the media and many prominent Democrats who either commend the group for being "antifascist" or pretend that Antifa doesn't exist. Rep, Jerry Nadler (D—New York), stated that "violence from Antifa" was a myth. But Andy Ngo has found the truth that Antifa is indeed a violent group. Ngo, in an interview with PJ Media, stated that "Antifa was able to move to the mainstream aided by new liberal allies because collectively they all had a shared enemy: Donald Trump," [104] Antifa convinced themselves that Trump was Hitler and they needed to respond or face a new Holocaust.

Andy Ngo tells of Mike Strickland, the first journalist attacked by Antifa. When Strickland defended himself against Antifa in Portland in 2016 with a legal concealed weapon, he was the one arrested and sent to jail. He did not fire a shot, so this was an obvious miscarriage of justice.

Strickland's arrest showed that the leftist establishment in Portland was protecting Antifa. It also sent a message that violence worked and Antifa could get away with it. Andy Ngo himself would be beaten three years later nearly to death and just this year, he was beaten a second time by Antifa. As he was getting beaten, Antifa merely laughed out loud. Andy Ngo was attacked by national publications as a racist extremist and many on the left excused Antifa's brutality. Ngo pointed out the symbiotic relationship between Antifa and left-wing groups like the Southern Poverty Law Center who would put Antifa targets on their own enemies list including Andy Ngo, whose only crime is telling the truth about Antifa and BLM. Andy Ngo observed, "For their world to live and thrive, America has to die." [105]

Damages between May 26 and June 8, 2020 resulted in as much as two billion dollars paid in insurance claims. In Minneapolis alone, 1500 buildings were destroyed. Minneapolis continues to be the costliest civil disorder in 2020-21 and much of the damage took place in minority communities on whose behalf they rioted for. Violent riots in Kenosha, Wisconsin left 50 million dollars in damages and nearly 60 buildings destroyed. The biggest damage occurred in the city's most diverse areas that included where most minorities lived. Like Chicago and Minneapolis, minority areas were the hardest hits in the Kenosha riots.

Costliest U.S. civil disorders

Includes riots and civil disorders causing insured losses to the insurance industry

Dates	Location	Dollars	2020 dollars
May 26-June 8, 2020	20 states across U.S.	$1-2b	$1-2b
Apr. 29-May 4, 1992	Los Angeles, CA	775m	1.42b
Aug. 11-17, 1965	Los Angeles, CA	44m	357m
Jul. 23, 1967	Detroit, MI	42m	322m
May 17-19, 1980	Miami, Fl	65m	204m
Apr. 4-9, 1968	Washington, DC	24m	179m
Jul. 13-14, 1977	New York, NY	28m	118m
Jul. 12. 1967	Newark, NJ	15m	115m
Apr. 6-9, 1968	Baltimore, MD	14m	104m
Apr. 4-11, 1968	Chicago, IL	13m	97m

Many Black Lives Matter and Antifa activists do not really care about the damage they cause since buildings and goods are just property—and not *their* property. Vicky Osterweil, author of *In Defense of Looting*, told NPR that it was morally justified for Black people to rob stores because "The very basis of property is derived through violence and through Black oppression…Looting strikes at the heart of property, of whiteness, and the police."[106] What these Democrat-sanctioned riots did was to destroy businesses that drive the economies of these urban centers, blocking chances for the poor to climb the economic ladder.

The Foundation for Economic Education's Brad Polumbo observed, "Callous disregard of property rights creates long-term instability that scares away business investment and reduces economic opportunity. Often, this manifests itself in the form of lower property values, consumers, reduced tax revenue, and <u>fewer jobs in an area</u>, "You don't have to just take my word for it. Studies examining the long-term economic impact of the <u>1960s Civil Rights Era riots</u> and the <u>1990s Los Angeles Rodney King riots</u> document these exact effects." [107]

Much of the rioters engaged in looting claimed Black Lives Matter as their rationale for destroying the inner-city communities they claim they are supporting. In the aftermath of the nationwide protests following the death of George Floyd as Kamala Harris told Stephen Colbert, about protesters, "They're not going to stop. They're not going to stop. This is a movement, I'm telling you. They're not going to stop, and everyone beware because they're not going to stop. They're not going to stop before Election Day and they're not going to stop after Election Day. And everyone should take note of that... They're not going to let up and **they should not.**"[108]

But she didn't just top there but chipped in a group called MN Freedom fund to help bail out those "protesting" on the ground.

Vice President Harris supported a fund that freed violent criminals rioting on the streets of Minneapolis. One local news station noted that those that Harris called for freeing included a suspect who shot at the police, a woman accused of killing a friend, and a sex offender. The Vice President raised money for violent rioters and while she later in the election "condemned violence", neither she nor President Biden ever mention Antifa or condemned the group by name. This merely showed that Antifa has become the black shirt thugs for the Democratic Party.

Kamala Harris ✔
@KamalaHarris

If you're able to, chip in now to the @MNFreedomFund to help post bail for those protesting on the ground in Minnesota.

Donate to the Minnesota Freedom Fund
Your support will help post bail for those protesting on the ground in Minnesota.
🔗 secure.actblue.com

4:34 PM · Jun 1, 2020 · Sprout Social

4.5K Retweets and comments   **2.2K** Likes

While the media intensively covered the January 6th Capitol riot, the reality is that at least 95% of riots in 2020 were linked to Black Lives Matter and we are talking one study that looked at a four-month period and saw three to four violent actions somewhere in the United States throughout the summer of 2020, pretty much from the left. One study conducted by Armed Conflict Location and Event Data Project (ACLED), found that 95% of riots in which there was information available involved Black Lives Matter. This study was originally designed to minimize violent activities conducted by the left yet; they produced overwhelming evidence that the left was responsible for *the vast majority of violent activities* in the summer of 2020.[109]

In a discussion about Antifa in the summer of 2019, I had liberal friends arguing that Antifa was not comparable to the various Neo Nazis and white supremacists, and one even mention they are "anti-fascist" since they have it in their name. Among the data I used to counter the "peaceful nature" of Antifa was 32 reported incidence of violence this group had done, including at least six attacks on journalists covering them. They were right, Antifa is not the equal of these supremacists or racists, they are worse. As Andy Ngo noted in his book *Unmasked,* they are well-trained para-militia who know self-defense and how to use weapons plus they have a political movement covering for them. When the right-wing rioters went into the U.S. Capitol, they were universally condemned by the conservative movement and no major political party supports rightwing extremists and neo-Nazis, but there are political movements that work with Antifa and support them. In Democratic-controlled cities like Portland and Seattle, they are allowed free reign to do what they want when they want. They call the tune while their left-wing patrons merely look on.[110]

Antifa in many ways are the spear used by the left to intimidate and strike fear in not just their opponents but in some cases people who are presumably their allies. How many times have Antifa threatened Portland Mayor Ted Wheeler, who all but gave them the key to the city? Wheeler, who appeased Antifa, found his own home under siege and was forced to move after radicals attacked him. Wheeler's email to his neighbors stated that is was "best for me and for everyone else's safety and peace to find a new place to live. I want to express my sincere apologies for the damage to our home and the fear that you are experiencing due to my position. It's unfair to all of you have no role in politics or my administration." [111]

Eoin Lenihan, writing in Quilletne, observed about the media apology for Antifa, "And yet, Antifa often receives media coverage that is neutral or even favorable, with its members' violence either being ignored by reporters or vaguely explained away as a product of right-wing provocation. What's more, anecdotal evidence has suggested that many of the mainstream reporters who are most active in covering Antifa also tend to enthusiastically amplify Antifa's claims on social media."[112]

Lenihan noted that there were reporters working for mainstream media outlets often produced favorable coverage for Antifa. Among those who apologized for Antifa was Jason Wilson, a Portland based reporter who contributes to Britain's *The Guardian*. Wilson often took the Antifa side on street violence and often quoted Mark Bray, who authored the "Antifa: The Anti-Fascist Handbook" as his source on the Antifa. Lenihan observed about one Wilson article, "In another column for *The Guardian*, this one about the 2018 "Occupy ICE" protest in Portland, Wilson quoted "local activist" Luis Marquez to the effect that "I think this occupation is a beautiful thing, a wonderful thing. Every single person here is a hero." Marquez is in fact a prominent Antifa leader in Portland, and has been arrested on numerous occasions due to his militant behavior—including alleged theft and assault"[113]

Many Portland journalists have been assaulted and harassed by Antifa whereas Wilson could easily mingle among Antifa and has supported Antifa tactics including doxxing and stalking to attack enemies of Antifa. Lenihan noted about Christopher Mathias of Huffington Post, "applies the same cynical approach. Like Wilson, Mathias' byline seems to pop up whenever Antifa stages violent protests—and he always can be counted on to deliver a play-by-play that favors Antifa. But he goes even further than his *Guardian* counterpart. Unlike Wilson, Mathias actually doxes individuals whom he suspects of being right-wing extremists. His doxing sources for an <u>article</u> about suspected extremists in the U.S. military included *Unicorn Riot*, an anarchic Antifa journalist collective, and other shady sites that exist as a sort of in-house *4chan* for the Antifa movement. (Mathias cited similar sources when he <u>published</u> identifying details of a Texas schoolteacher, and of a <u>Virginia police officer</u>.)" [114]

While the media has covered the January 6th riot with intensity, they often downplayed violence of the left. To reinforce the left's violence part in attacking their opponents, one incident reported by WBZ in Boston involved seven masked people who were arrested after they attacked a small group of pro-life supporters in the summer of 2019 and threw urine at one of the speakers.

For the past four years, Antifa and other leftist street gangs have kept conservative speakers from speaking at college, "countered" conservatives' rallies, and marches, and struck terror while destroying urban centers in the name of social justice. And Democrats like Mayor Wheeler in Portland have appeased Antifa and throughout the United States, many Democratic cities did very little to stop the riots but instead defunded or cut the police budget, resulting in increased violent crimes in these cities. Minneapolis decided to hire new police officers at the beginning of 2021 when it appeared their appeasements of rioters created a spike in violent crime. The irony is that Antifa and BLM movement riots destroyed many minority communities and when the police were defunded, it was minority communities who felt the brunt of increased crime. Antifa are a domestic terrorist' group and in 2020, street violence was the result of leftist gangs and a major political party that was prepared to ignore the violence since it served their purpose, in promoting leftist policies, and helping to elect Joe Biden.

Media Class: An Appendage of the Democratic Party and Political Left

The media is biased toward Democrats. True and enough data to back that up but the real problem where does one go for truth or at least a non-partisan view of the news?

In March of 2021, Judge Laurence Silberman single out media bias in his dissent in *Tah v Global Witness* dealing with how much protection the media should receive in dealing with defamation. The Supreme Court has given the media wide leeway in protecting them from defamation in *New York Times v Sullivan* but in this case, Silberman called for the reformation of defamation laws approved by the courts and beginning with the evolution of much of the media including the *New York Times* and *Washington Post* into what he described as "Democratic Party broadsheets" and adding that the news section of the *Wall Street Journal* has followed suit. Most major broadcast and cable outlets along with Big Tech are not much different from the *New York Times*, Judge Silberman cautioned. with their reporters nothing more than "Democratic operatives with byline."

From Judge Silberman's dissent, "One can understand, if not approve, the Supreme Court's policy-driven decision. There can be no doubt that the *New York Times* case has increased the power of the media. Although the institutional press, it could be argued, needed that protection to cover the civil rights movement, that power is now abused. In light of today's very different challenges, I doubt the Court would invent the same ruled, As the case has subsequently been interpreted, it allows the press to cast false aspersions on public figures with near impunity. It would be one thing if this were a two-sided phenomenon. Cf. *New York Times*, 376 U.S. at 305 (Goldberg, J., concurring) (reasoning that the press will publish the responses of public officials to reports or accusations). But see Suzanne Garment, *The Culture of Mistrust in American Politics* 74–75, 81–82 (1992) (noting that the press more often manufactures scandals involving political conservatives). The increased power of the press is so dangerous today because we are very close to one-party control of these institutions. Our court was once concerned about the institutional consolidation of the press leading to a "bland and homogenous" marketplace of ideas. See *Hale v. FCC*, 425 F.2d 556, 562 (D.C. Cir. 1970) (Tamm, J., concurring). It turns out that ideological consolidation of the press (helped along by economic consolidation) is the far greater threat… Although the bias against the Republican Party—not just controversial individuals—is rather shocking today, this is not new; it is a long-term, secular trend going back at least to the '70s. (I do not mean to defend or criticize the behavior of any particular politician). Two of the three most influential papers (at least historically), The *New York Times* and the *Washington Post*, are virtually Democratic Party broadsheets. And the news section of the *Wall Street Journal* leans in the same direction. The orientation of these three papers is followed by the Associated Press and most large papers across the country (such as the *Los Angeles Times*, *Miami Herald*, and *Boston Globe*). Nearly all television—network and cable—is a Democratic Party trumpet. Even the government-supported National Public Radio follows along…As has become apparent, Silicon Valley also has an enormous influence over the distribution of news. And it similarly filters news delivery in ways favorable to the Democratic Party. See Kaitlyn Tiffany, <u>Twitter Goofed It</u>, *The Atlantic* (2020) ("Within a few hours, Facebook announced that it would limit [a *New York Post*] story's spread on its platform while its third-party fact-checkers somehow investigated the information. Soon after, Twitter took an even more dramatic stance: Without immediate public explanation, it completely banned users from posting the link to the story.")."[115]

About the impact of this bias, he warned, "To be sure, there are a few notable exceptions to Democratic Party ideological control: Fox News, the *New York Post*, and the *Wall Street Journal*'s editorial page. It should be sobering for those concerned about news bias that these institutions are controlled by a single man and his son. Will a lone holdout remain in what is otherwise a frighteningly orthodox media culture? After all, there are serious efforts to muzzle Fox News. And although upstart (mainly online) conservative networks have emerged in recent years, their visibility has been decidedly curtailed by social media, either by direct bans or content-based censorship...There can be little question that the overwhelming uniformity of news bias in the United States has an enormous political impact. That was empirically and persuasively demonstrated in Tim Groseclose's insightful book, *Left Turn: How Liberal Media Bias Distorts the American Mind* (2011). Professor Groseclose showed that media bias is significantly to the left. Id. at 192–197; see also id. at 169–77. And this distorted market has the effect, according to Groseclose, of aiding Democratic Party candidates by 8–10% in the typical election. Id. at ix, 201–33. And now, a decade after this book's publication, the press and media do not even pretend to be neutral news services...It should be borne in mind that the first step taken by any potential authoritarian or dictatorial regime is to gain control of communications, particularly the delivery of news. It is fair to conclude, therefore, that one-party control of the press and media is a threat to a viable democracy. It may even give rise to countervailing extremism. The First Amendment guarantees a free press to foster a vibrant trade in ideas. But a biased press can distort the marketplace. And when the media has proven its willingness—if not eagerness—to so distort, it is a profound mistake to stand by unjustified legal rules that serve only to enhance the press' power."[116]

This bias threatens the ability for all thoughts to be equally entertained and making the media an extension of the political class that determines the narrative on most issues. As we have seen, much of the scientific debate dealing with key issues are not even allowed to part of the general discussion as many who disagree with the "conventional wisdom" on issues on climate change or with how to deal with the Wuhan virus, *were often treated as deniers despite that much of their science proved to be correct!* The media failure to cover both sides or allow dissenters to be part of the debate, had its consequences including supporting policies that proved economically disastrous and will end up killing more people than saving. Judge Silberman, quoting Professor Groseclose's book *Left Turn*, shows that this bias has aided Democrats by an 8 to 10% in the typical election.

Professor Groseclose himself in his book detailed a study for instance, one study, conducted by Yale researchers Alan Gerber, Ethan Kaplan. and Daniel Bergan, "recruited hundreds of subjects in the Northern Virginia suburbs of Washington, D.C. They bought them subscriptions to The Washington Post or The Washington Times. (And randomly chose, which subjects would receive which subscription… Northern Virginia, the researchers gave trial subscriptions to the *Washington Post*. To another set, they gave trial subscriptions to the *Washington Times,,,*Gerber and his coauthors found that in the gubernatorial race they examined, their

Washington Post-subscribing subjects voted 3.8 percentage points higher for the Democratic candidate than did their *Washington Times*-subscribing subjects. Given that the *Post* adopts a more liberal slant than the *Times*, the result suggests that newspapers really do influence the way people do think and vote.[117]

"After aggregating the results of this and similar studies," Groseclose adds, "one finds an inescapable conclusion: Newspapers, television, radio and online media are extremely influential, especially over consumers' political views." [118]

Groseclose found that the media is expressed not just through distortion of facts but the omission of facts. One example was the Bush tax cuts in 2003, when he noted, "All the liberals were saying that under this tax plan the very rich are going to get a highly disproportionate share of the benefits, and that was true — something like the top 1 percent would get 30 to 35 percent of the total tax cuts. But one fact a lot of media people didn't mention is that the reason that was true is that the very rich pay most of the taxes. When Reagan did his tax cut, he just said, 'We're going to take whatever you pay in taxes, and we're going to multiply it by 0.75, and everyone's going to get 25 percent off what they usually pay... The Bush Plan is actually going to have a bigger percentage cut for the poorest people.' What that meant was that after taxes were cut, the rich would actually be paying a *higher* percentage of overall taxes than before. The Bush tax cut actually made the tax more progressive. So, there are two facts that are equally true, but one was the fact that all the liberals were talking about, and the other was the fact all the conservatives were talking about." [119]

In the 2020 elections, much of the media refuse to cover Hunter Biden's history of profiting from his father's position including deals done with the Chinese. When the *New York Post* broke the story, social media tech refuse to allow this story from being passed around and Twitter locked the *New York Post*'s account.

In one post-election survey from the Media Research Center and the Polling Company, voters in seven swing states (Arizona, Georgia, Michigan, Nevada, North Carolina, Pennsylvania and Wisconsin), were asked eight key issues including Hunter Biden's assault allegations, Hunter Biden scandals, Kamala Harris's leftist voting record, the third quarter economic growth of 33% and the economic job creation from May 2020, Middle East peace deals and US energy independence. Eighty-two percent of voters were unaware of least one of these stories and 17% of the voters admitted they would have changed their votes had they known. This may have been enough to swing the elections, supporting Justice Silverman's dissent that this overwhelming bias benefitted Democrats. [120]

POST-ELECTION SURVEY OF 1,750 BIDEN VOTERS IN 7 SWING STATES		Percent Unaware	Shift Away from Biden
	Biden Sex Assault Allegations	35.4%	8.9%
	Hunter Biden Scandal	45.1%	9.4%
	Harris Most Leftist Senator	25.3%	4.1%
	33.1% Economic Growth	49.0%	5.6%
	Created 11.1 Million Jobs	39.4%	5.4%
	Middle East Peace Deals	43.5%	5.0%
	U.S. Energy Independence	50.5%	5.8%
	Operation Warp Speed	36.1%	5.3%
	TOTAL (Unaware of at least one)	82%	17%

mrc Based on MRC/Polling Company survey of 1,750 actual Biden voters in AZ, GA, MI, NV, NC, PA and WI. Nov 9-18, 2020

Throughout Trump's term, there were numerous times in which the media provided wrong information from the Charlottesville riot of 2017, when they denied that Trump condemned Nazis and white nationalists, the fake news that Trump was briefed that

Russian military intelligence paid Afghan Taliban bounties, the bogus *Atlantic* smears that Trump called troops who died in battle "losers" and "suckers" which lasted only 48 hours when a dozen witnesses—including John Bolton who left the administration after he made clear his opposition to Trump and his policies—debunked the story. Then there was the Trump tax return story in which it was claimed in one year he only paid $750 in taxes, but in reality, as pundit Stephen Green observed, "Trump has paid enough in taxes just this century to buy more than one $85 million F-35A Lightning II stealth strike jet."[121]

Then there is the grandfather of all fake stories, the "Russian collusion" hoax in which Trump colluded with Russia to win in 2016. Not only was this story false, but the Obama-Biden administration never had any empirical evidence that Russian agents coordinated with the Trump campaign. This story would have a dramatic impact on the Trump administration, as Trump was under siege from an independent counsel investigation of a crime that never happened. Much of the media failed to correct the record and failed to apologize for this fake story whose fraud was obvious as late as 2019 when the Mueller Report was published.

Sharyl Attkisson listed 152 false or misleading statements about the Trump administration on her website, which gives you an idea how bad the reporting was during the Trump era. Studies from the conservative Media Research Center, NPR, and the left of center Pew Research Center reported that 90%-95% of stories about Trump administration were negative. One study found that there was one positive story about President Trump for every eight positive stories about President Obama. One can argue that Trump had his failures but a honest review of Trump's presidency would show that his administration had more accomplishments in four years than Obama did in eight, including increasing job creation and increased income for the middle class, minorities and the lower class, Middle East peace deals between Sunni Arabs and Israel, and cutting unemployment in half during the pandemic recession in spite of the lockdowns imposed by many Democrat governors. The Trump administration should also get credit for Operation Warp Speed, which produced three vaccines in record time. You can debate Trump's policies or his personality, but you can't debate that maybe a few more positive stories could have been written about his achievements. That 95% of the stories about President Trump were negative shows that the media class has gone beyond bias into being an affiliate of the Democratic Party.

As we saw from the Media Research Center survey and from Judge Silberman's dissent, when the media fails to do its basic service to inform the public, it is a threat to America. The importance of freedom of the press is to ensure that we have available media that is willing to report negatively on the government and be part of the mechanism that produces accountability from those in power. When the media essentially acts as a propaganda arm for the state and becomes a tool of the government, then freedom is threatened including freedom of the press for those who opposes the status quo become the target.

Narrowing the spectrum of permissible opinion is being done with the cooperation of Big Tech and the Democratic Party. The censorship of stories dealing with Hunter Biden was one way the Tech's companies aided the Democrats in the 2020 election. They acted as "fact checkers," which often favored the Left's version of truth as opposed to the truth. They have not only purged conservatives' voices on their sites, but they also helped push an alternative social media site, Parler, off of the major tech networks. This use of monopoly power by Big Tech was directed not just as Parler, but also conservative voices in general as Parler provided a home for many conservatives.

Social media reaches billions throughout the world and many younger people, social media is their primary source of news. With 70 percent of Americans having a social media account, Big Tech companies like Twitter and Facebook have become the number one source of communication today and many increased their viewing of social media during the pandemic. About 40 billion dollars were spent on ads on social media in 2020 and this is expected to increase nearly 20% in 2021.

Big Tech has become a major sector of our economy, with the ability to determine the social discourse, and they are now creating the new norms of what views will be and not be acceptable. As we have seen, Big Tech has the ability to block certain news stories from appearing. Big Tech platforms have the unchecked ability to censor and edit whatever they want, giving them more control than any other media have ever had. When Twitter and Facebook can arbitrarily ban a former president from their platforms, we should be concerned even if we don't like the former president or his policies.

Heartland Institute fellow Samantha Fillmore noted, "This issue of censorship and proxy editing is significant and should be treated as such. Legislators should consider solutions that would protect all Americans from undue censorship by a cabal of Big Tech ideologues who wield near-total power over the dissemination of information in today's social media-dominated environment. Social media is the modern-day public square, and in America, everyone has a right to voice their opinion, regardless of whether or not a few tech titans agree with their views. More speech, not less speech, is always better in a free society." [122]

The political left wants complete censorship of their opponents, so they continually attack major news conservative news networks, including Fox News, Newsmax, and One America News Network. About Fox and other conservative networks, Brian Stelter, of CNN said, "Do these private companies have too much power? Sure, and many people would say 'Yes, of course,' But reducing a liar's reach is not the same as censoring freedom of speech. Freedom of speech is different than freedom of reach. And algorithmic reach is part of the problem." Stelter is calling for his competitors to be censored and removed from the public square.

The Federalist culture editor Emily Jashinsky observed, "Silicon Valley's interests involve melting our brains to buy more hoodies. They want money—lots of it—and they've spent a decade proving their willingness to hurt the public in pursuit of that goal. When they've taken their cues from Stelter and his fellow neoliberal pearl-clutchers in the past, it's been in the service of public relations which, again, is just about money…If Stelter thinks that will always be the case, he is sorely mistaken. Then again, the corporate press has been so successful at bullying Big Tech and other industries into disseminating bourgeois progressivism, they lose sight of the 30,000-foot view, which is a sprawling new infrastructure in the hands of irresponsible corporatists built to enforce whatever political narrative they choose…Stelter's flavor of media criticism is breathless and without nuance. Sure, it's progressive, but it's not really well-argued. It's just the sort of reflexive outrage over which CNN claims to criticize Fox, but ultimately does better than anyone else…That's reason enough not to take Stelter seriously, but at this point, other journalists at legacy outlets should be pushing back hard on the shortsighted policies Stelter is using his platform to sell under the banner of responsible journalism. They are dangerous to the free press and will eventually hurt everyone in media, but also the public that relies on us for information."[123]

Once Social Media giants gain control of all political discourse, it is over for any member of the media who dares to challenge the giants' views. Stelter's own view is short sighted since he is assuming since Big Tech oligarchies will not turn on him and his network. Social media has become the enforcer in making sure that the leftist narrative dominates, from climate change and other scientific debates to political discussion. The threat to free speech is obvious. As we move closer to the road to serfdom, Big Tech will eventually tell us which thoughts will be allowed and will not.

From the Antifa street thugs to Big Tech's boardrooms, the left is now moving for complete control of what is considered acceptable speech, and once that is done, they will control not just the political debate but the culture itself.

Rise of Oil and Natural Gas as Our Weapon

T he past four years, the increase in American energy production is one of those economic miracles not thought possible a decade ago. Oil and gas production will reduce the United
States' dependence on imported energy, and we may become
an energy exporter, strengthening our international status. The
rise of domestic energy production was done despite the Obama
Administration, which tried to slow increases in oil and natural
gas production via fracking.

As Manhattan Institute fellow Mark P. Mills notes, *"Growth in
natural gas has made America the world's largest producer and could
soon make us a huge exporter. In the past half-dozen years, America's
hydrocarbon juggernaut has boosted our economy by hundreds of
dollars."*[124] Mills argued noted that there are some myths about
America's energy boom that need to be dispelled. One of these is
that Big Oil is the biggest benefactor of the U.S.'s increased energy
production. He notes that 75% of our oil and natural gas production comes from 20,000 small and midsize oil and gas firms with
an average size of 15 employees.

The oil and natural gas boom are part of a larger tech boom as
it is dependent on what Mills describes as *"The emergence of infor-
mation-centric 'smart' drilling, which relies on sensors, computers*

and control systems that, when combined with steerable horizontal drilling, fracking and a skilled work force, created the boom." [125]

This boom spread throughout the country. North Dakota became a job mecca. Texas's economic growth has been aided by its energy industry. But jobs have been created in many states, such as Pennsylvania, Florida, Illinois, and Ohio. (New York has banned fracking, another example of Andrew Cuomo incompetence and lack of concern for the people he supposedly serves.)

California ranks behind Texas in energy production and potential. Many of these states support Democrats and this energy revolution has the potential to lift these states out of their economic doldrums. (Unfortunately, California governor Gavin Newsom has been determined to ensure that his state fails to develop its natural resources and instead relies on more expensive and less dependable green technology.)

For every energy production job created in the field, there are three or four jobs created in office-based blue- and white-collar jobs. This has led to foreign firms investing $166 billion in American energy. More importantly, these energy-related jobs can't be exported overseas!

Energy-related economic growth isn't just limited to oil and gas production; hydrocarbon manufacturing, including petroleum refining and extraction, has grown 40% for the past six years and these new plants have generated 600,000 jobs. Fossil fuels production jobs are better paying than renewable energy ones, and you can't move an oil field or natural gas field to China.

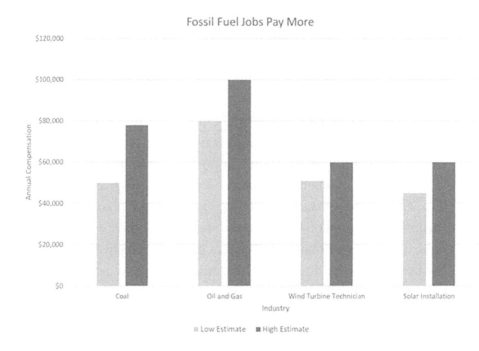

Fossil Fuel Jobs Pay More

The key obstacle to this energy-related boom is federal government policy, the final obstacle will be environmental extremists pushing regulations through many stats, such as the fracking bans that have taken place in New York, Maryland, and Vermont. Further bans and restrictions will take place in other blue states and nationally as a part of the Green New Deal.

The energy boom has caused. the United States, along with Mexico and Canada, now has the potential of being the world's leading energy giant, neutralizing OPEC and allowing the United States more leeway in foreign affairs. The Biden plan will make us more dependent upon Middle East while increasing the cost of energy at home.

Nicholas Eberstadt, Derek Scissors and Evan Abramsky observed, "Regardless of whether the U.S. is a slight importer or exporter, its current petroleum profile has fundamentally changed the geopolitical facts. The strategic importance of Middle Eastern oil exports for U.S. national interests has suffered a major-league downgrade. The biggest loser here may be the House of Saud, with which Washington now has far less need to make any devil's bargains. Between 2006 and 2019, the volume of U.S. crude-oil imports from the kingdom fell by 60 percent. Any prospective Iranian petro-leverage over the U.S. has also been quashed. The tired insinuation that U.S. policy in the Middle East is grounded in oil covetousness looks more detached from reality than ever. Needless to say, the U.S. still retains important interests in the Middle East, but whatever the American role in the Middle East should be, it no longer *must* be primarily driven by oil... FORTUNATELY for President Biden, he has inherited an economy that has already grown ever more petroleum-efficient over the past four decades and is on track to continue to do so, barring any egregious policy blunders...One of the key fault lines for such green policy-making runs through China. If fracking is curbed, either our petroleum independence will vanish, or our domestic green-energy output must soar. The latter option will be much more difficult, protracted, and expensive if the PRC's heavily subsidized green-energy industry is not allowed to participate meaningfully in our domestic market. But large-scale Chinese participation would subject America." [126]

Energy independence has given the United States flexibility in its policy in the Middle East and if we move away from this energy policy, we become more dependent not just on the Middle East but also on China as our "green technology" become yet another aspect of businesses and jobs headed toward China.

Trump: The Beginning
of Realpolitik

T rump's foreign policy was a return to *realpolitik* based on a balance-of-power view of the world. Michael Barone noted, *"Some will dismiss his appointments and tweets as expressing no more than the impulses of an ignorant and undisciplined temperament — no more premeditated than the lunges of a rattlesnake. Others may recall that similar things were said (by me, as well as many others) about his campaign strategy. But examination of the entrails of the election returns suggests that Trump was following a deliberate strategy based on shrewd insight when he risked antagonizing white college-educated voters in the process of appealing to non-college-educated whites."* [127]

Historian and Hoover Institution fellow Niall Ferguson views Trump's foreign policy as an extension of Henry Kissinger's worldview. He observed, *"A world run by regional great powers with strong men in command, all of whom understand that any lasting international order must be based on the balance of power."* [128]

As Michael Barone notes, Trump took a congratulatory call for his election victory from Taiwan's president. Tsai Ing-wen. The first visit to Trump Tower after the election was Japanese Prime Minister Shinzo Abe; this sent a message that China would not be allowed to operate in the Western Pacific unchallenged and Trump would work with our allies. Trump also appointed Terry Branstad, the governor of Iowa, as the ambassador to China. Branstad first met Xi Jinping in 1985. Barone viewed the appointment as a "bad cop, good cop" move. He observed, *"Trump wants some changes in trade relations with China and limits on its probes in the South China Sea and will build up U.S. military forces. But there's room for acceptance of China as a great power. Trump wants some changes in trade relations with China and limits on its probes in the South China Sea and will build up U.S. military forces."* [129]

As for dealing with Russia, Barone added, *"There's room for acceptance of Russia, too, as suggested by the secretary-of-state nomination of Exxon Mobil CEO Rex Tillerson, self-proclaimed friend of Russian president Vladimir Putin's. He may be opposed by Republican senators who, like Mitt Romney in 2012, see Russia as "our No. 1 geopolitical foe." But perhaps Trump favors Kissinger's proposal for a neutral and decentralized (i.e., dominated and partitioned) Ukraine, with an end to sanctions on Russia. Tillerson would be a good choice if that were your goal. This would make the Baltic States and Poland understandably nervous, but they could take some comfort in Trump's reaffirmation of our NATO pledge to defend them and in the fact that Pentagon nominee James Mattis has gone out of his way to honor Estonia for its sacrifices in Iraq and Afghanistan."* [130] The irony that Barone was not entirely correct as Trump proved tougher on Putin than the Obama-Biden administration ever was,

Trump's criticism of NATO included his view that NATO member states should contribute more toward their own defenses. This may have seen results. As Michael Barone noted, *"Finance ministers, stung by Trump's campaign criticisms, are ponying up more money to meet their NATO defense-spending commitments; German chancellor Angela Merkel is backing down from her disastrous decision to welcome 1 million refugees."* [131]

Brexit was the first break in the European Union's dominance of the continent. While Obama threatened Britain with being sent to the "back of the queue" if they voted to leave the EU, Trump supported Brexit and a possible future U.S-U.K. free trade agreement. Brexit could be the first step toward the formation of the Anglosphere an alliance of English-speaking nations that would support Trump's "America First" view of the world.

In the Middle East, Trump ditched Iranian deal and boosted the Sunni-Israeli alliance against increasing Iranian influence through various peace agreements between Sunni states and Israel. While Trump may pay less lip service to human rights, the reality is that Obama also paid lip service to human rights.

Niall Ferguson noted, *"Yet it was Trump who in August (2016) pledged that his Administration would "speak out against the oppression of women, gays and people of different faith" in the name of Islam. While the Obama Administration has shunned proponents of Islamic reform, Trump pledged to "be a friend to all moderate Muslim reformers in the Middle East, and [to] amplify their voices. This includes speaking out against the horrible practice of honor killings," as well as establishing as "one of my first acts as President . . . a Commission on Radical Islam which will include reformist voices in the Muslim community."* [132]

Ferguson's point is that Trump did not make human rights a central theme of his foreign policy but his policy against Iran in the Middle East and China did more to advance human rights than the Obama/Biden administration did. President Obama often *talked* about the importance of human rights, but the Obama administration often ignored helping the truly suffering. His Syria policy may be responsible for the death of a half million Syrians, not to mention the thousands of people who died in Iraq and other Middle East nations because of Obama's reckless policies.

In 1982, Herman Kahn wrote *The Coming Boom,* in which he foresaw the economic prosperity of the Reagan years and a new world order that included the rise of regional powers and new challenges to the bipolar power struggle between the United States and the U.S.S.R. Kahn thought that a multipolar world would eventually stabilize but the era before stabilization could be chaotic. Kahn's predictions proved to be accurate.

Kahn saw the rise of China, Japan, and Germany as powers. Today, Germany is the leading European economic power and Russia is working on expanding its sphere of influence within Central Europe while reestablishing Russian nationalism. China is working on being a Pacific power and both Russia and China look to check American power. After the collapse of the Soviet Empire, the United States was the lone superpower, but Russia, China, Germany, and India are now looking for their own place in the world as global powers. The rise of these countries signifies that we live in a multipolar world.

The Trump Administration's goal was to challenge our loyalty to transnational organizations, beginning with the United Nations. *If one is serious about foreign policy, you can't be serious about the United Nations, but if you are serious about the United Nations, you can't be serious about foreign policy.* When Obama failed to veto a UN resolution condemning Israel after the 2016 election, this reminded many Americans and most Republicans of the anti-American and anti-Israeli attitude of much of the United Nations. Obama's support of the Iran nuclear deal allowed Iran to increase their influence in the Middle East.

Lawrence Sondhaus in his book *World War One: The Global Revolution* discussed the debate about the U.S. joining the League of Nations and how the Republicans in the Senate failed to ratify Woodrow Wilson's vision of transnational collective security. Sondhaus observed that while Sen. Henry Cabot Lodge opposed the League of Nations, he favored an active foreign policy that defended American interests in a way like what President Theodore Roosevelt followed during his administration. Lodge supported a separate treaty that promised France that the United States and Great Britain would defend her, since Lodge perceived this treaty as being in our national interest. Wilson's refusal to separate the debate over whether America should join the League of Nations from the issue of America signing the Versailles Treaty doomed United States support for the Versailles Treaty. A similar debate will soon begin about America's involvement in transnational organizations such as the United Nations and whether it is in our national interest to stay in or at least be as active in these organizations as in the past. Trump 's "America first" foreign policy didn't mean isolationism, but a foreign policy that defends America's interest first.

Anne Bayefsky, director of the Touro Institute for Human Rights and the Holocaust, stated about the 2016 UN resolutions about Israel, "Let's be absolutely clear about what has just happened. *The Palestinians have completed the hijacking of every major UN institution. The 2016 General Assembly has adopted nineteen resolutions condemning Israel and nine critical of all other UN states combined. The 2016 Commission on the Status of Women adopted one resolution condemning Israel and zero on any other state. The 2016 UN Human Rights Council celebrated ten years of adopting more resolutions and decisions condemning Israel than any other place on earth. And now – to the applause of the assembled – the Palestinians can add the UN Security Council to their list...*Resolution sponsors Malaysia and New Zealand explained UN-think to the Council this way: Israeli settlements are "the single biggest threat to peace" and the "primary threat to the viability of the two-state solution." Not seven decades of unremitting Arab terror and violent rejection of Jewish self-determination in the* *historic homeland of the Jewish people...At its core, this UN move is a head-on assault on American democracy. President Obama knew full well he did not have Congressional support for the Iran deal, so he went straight to the Security Council first. Likewise, he knew that there would have been overwhelming Congressional opposition to this resolution, so he carefully planned his stealth attack... He waited until Congress was not in session. Members of his administration made periodic suggestions that nothing had been decided. There were occasional head fakes that he was "leaning" against it. He produced smiling photo-ops from a Hawaiian golf course with no obvious major foreign policy moves minutes away. Holiday time-outs were in full swing across the country. And then he pounced, giving Israel virtually no notice of his intent not to veto."* [133]

Trump was a good ally of Israel and did what others have promised but didn't do: move the US embassy to Jerusalem. While the professional diplomatic class stated that the move would prove disastrous, it not only didn't prove disastrous, but it didn't even stop Trump's biggest diplomatic coup, the Abraham Accords which allied Sunni Arabs with Israel. Trump didn't just ditch the Iran deal, but also designed the Abraham Accords as a strategic architecture to counter Iranian influence. The accords tied the interest of Sunni Arabs and Israel to counter, the Iranian threat. Prior to the Trump administration, Palestinians had veto power over American policy toward Israel. Trump's solution was to expand our national interest in the Middle East beyond the Palestinians conflict with Israel. Jared Kushner, Mike Pompeo, and Trump made sure the Palestinians did not get into the way of America's effort to counter the rise of Iran, a direct result of the Obama-Biden Iranian nuclear deal, one of many bad foreign policy decisions made by the Obama-Biden administration. If Biden returns the Palestinians to center stage in the Middle East, this could undermine the Abraham Accords and allow Iran to become the central

Biden's energy policy. Imposing new restrictions on American oil and gas production and distribution, plays into the hands of our enemies and OPEC, and reducing our options in the Middle East. The real problem of the Biden administration is that it is filled with former members of the Obama administration /whose Middle East policies proved to be a disaster to our national interest.

A second goal of American foreign policy is to strengthen our alliance against China. The Biden administration be challenged by a more aggressive China and any alliance against China will depend on how our allies view American strength.

Trump confronted Chinese Communist Party efforts for military dominance, advocated for pro-democracy activists and persecuted minorities. and. Most importantly leading a fight against Beijing's efforts to export authoritarian models, including adopting technological censorship the coopting of other nations' elites and institution including our own. Our foreign policy establishment has given special accommodations in trade, with the idea of exporting our values. But the Chinese are also exporting their values. Big Tech's censorship of conservative thoughts copies the Chinese social media's own censorship of its citizens Confucius Institutes impacts China's history is taught in our Universities.

One of the defenders of the old view of China is Joe Biden, whose families also benefitted from deals in China while he served as vice-president. The question is whether Biden has learned anything. At the beginning of his administration, there was no real deviation from Trump's foreign policies. How long this last is questionable, since the people Biden put in place to oversee in his foreign policy were. in the past was part of the old Chinese policy. During the election, Biden conceded that China was our biggest competitor, but that Russia was our bigger threat. Before he left office, Trump imposed visa restrictions on individuals involved in their connections to foreign influence as well as limiting the length of visas for Chinese Communist Party (CCP) members to one month.

As *National Review* observed, "These narrowly tailored visa restrictions alleviated concerns that an all-encompassing ban on the CCP's more than 90 million members from entering the United States would sweep up ordinary people. Instead, this approach targets Party leaders, immediate family, and those who truly pose a threat. Contrary to Democrats' claims that such visa restrictions are racist and xenophobic, they demonstrate solidarity with the people of China against those most responsible for the ruling regime's human-rights atrocities." [134]Note that many Democrats view *any* restriction on Chinese diplomats as racist, which demonstrates how much many within our leadership class have absorbed Chinese values. Acting as if challenging China hegemony is racist is nonsense, since the Chinese are this century's National Socialist/ Fascist regime.

In the 1990's, a good friend told me about a few years after the collapse of the Soviet Empire that he was surprised how communism ended up as National Socialism. The Hitler of today is President Xi.

China has concentration camps that hold millions, they use social media to control the population and President Xi is the Big Brother of our time. There is no liberty in China, and while the CCP allows profits to be made, the state controls every "private" enterprise. It is state corporatism, and China controls business as tightly as Hitler did in Germany and Mussolini did in Italy. OK? China views itself as the new center of the universe, with all nations bow to Beijing. While I don't view China's, National socialism means conquering nations, there is one exception: to ensure that Chinese Communist ideology reigns supreme, freedom in Hong Kong and Taiwan must be crushed.

What will a world be like if China was the most powerful country? It would be a poorer and less free world. We will see what will happen when other nations or groups of nations copy China's national socialism. We will see more of own elites discuss their admiration of China the way Michael Bloomberg, for example, stated in the 2020 Democratic primary that "Well, it's a question of what is a dictator. *They don't have a democracy in the sense that they have general elections. That is true. They do have a system where a small group of people appoints the head. And they churn over periodically. If you go back and look at the last two or three decades, there have been a number of people that have had the same position that Xi Jinping has.*" [135]

But if China becomes the number one power, this means the United States will decline in economic power, and the freedom we take for granted will slowly disappear.

Trump's foreign policy team has put an alliance in place, the Quad partnership between Australia, India, Japan and United States. which was originally conceived in 2007 before being disbanded in 2008. This is becoming the nucleus of a multilateral response to Chinese moves into the Indian and Pacific Oceans. We are looking at moving from the demands of competition into a direct conflict with Beijing. AEI scholar H. W. Brands, noted, "Well into Barack Obama's presidency, U.S. cyber posture featured, with some very important exceptions, an emphasis on cultivating norms of restraint in this emerging domain of competition. The problem was that these norms were shared mostly by friendly democracies, but not by hostile autocracies…Russia and China, along with North Korea and Iran, have used cyberspace as an arena for hacking, espionage, and political meddling. Since 2017, U.S. Cyber Command has shifted to a more aggressive strategy featuring "persistent engagement" and "forward defense" — getting inside rivals' networks and using disruptive action, or at least the threat of it, to keep them off balance." [136]

Trump's policies, from energy policies and the Abraham Accords to the Quad alliances recalibrated foreign policy towards more traditional goals. Donald Trump s administration brought back *realpolitik*, in which our country's foreign policy will be based on America's national interest. Idealism will no longer be a reason to send young Americans into combat. but defending our national interest will.

The pandemic has exposed the failures of the EU as both United States and Great Britain have designed and produce vaccines in record time, and that both nations have, as of the spring of 2021, vaccinated far more people than the European Union has.

The weakness of the European Union is not the lack of creativity on the part of their people but the political institutions in place retard growth. Even in older European countries such as France and Germany, entrepreneurs are frustrated by bureaucratic inertia. In the United States, the Obama administration placed countless obstacles in the path of economic growth and Biden's economic plan is even worse when it came to planning new obstacles to entrepreneurship, following the failed EU policies. For four years, Trump administration unleashed the creativity of the private sector, which resulted in Operation Warp Speed and development of new vaccines. The biggest threat to the United States' continued prosperity will be the Biden Administration imitating the EU administrative state.

One solution for American foreign policy makers is the development of the Anglosphere. James C. Bennett and Michael J. Lotus in their book *America 3.0* saw the end of the bureaucratic state, or what they call "the end of America 2.0," and return to a smaller and more decentralized "America 3.0." Bennett and Lotus begin with a brief history of how we got to where we are at present, as we moved from being an agricultural America 1.0 to an industrial America 2.0. What Bennett and Lotus present is not just a roadmap toward a new America over the next25 years, but a new foreign policy based on the alliance of the Anglosphere nations: United States, Great Britain, Canada, Australia, and New Zealand. We are not yet close to America 3.0 that Bennett and Lotus envisioned, we do see an opportunity that Republican governors like Ron DeSantis move their states forward and as DeSantis showed in 2020, Republicans can move their own agenda in the face of obstacles imposed by a pandemic. This could be the beginning of an attack on the bureaucratic state.

Bennett and Lotus trace our roots and our desire for liberty and individualism back before 1776 to the Anglo-Saxon invaders in the fifth century after the fall of the Roman Empire. Our culture has two thousand years of history, and our desire for liberty is inherited. One thing that scholars see as a sign of progress is the nuclear family with individuals, not parents, selecting their spouse. The beginning of freedom for women began when this happened, and children left their parents' home and no longer belonged to extended families. From there, they made their own wealth and expanded the economic pie.

The question is whether we can move to an America 3.0 without a complete collapse. The authors say this can happen. They present a libertarian vision that includes the elimination of the federal income tax and dramatically reducing federal government power, but they still support a defensive posture that includes maintaining our present alliances, along with federal protections for civil rights. So, while the authors questioned much of our foreign policy for the past decade and their criticism mirrored Trump's, they don't call for the non-interventionist policy of Ron Paul or his son, Sen. Rand Paul. (Although Rand Paul might want to adopt their policies as his own.) They believe America should continue to protect trading routes, following a policy that Britain and America have done for three centuries.

On domestic policy, they see many of our social problems being created by the federal government and foreseeing many states forming regional compacts on policies like health care. While many conservatives and libertarians may not agree with their vision, Bennett and Lotus present both a domestic and foreign policy alternative that can be synergistic with Trump Populism and Reagan conservatism.

While European are attempting to build a bureaucratic, centralized European Union, the Anglosphere nations are for most part suspicious of top-down super state institutions and instead as Bennett and Lotus state, "promote more and stronger cooperative institutions, not to build some English-speaking super state on the European Union, or to annex Britain, Canada or Australia to the United States but rather to protect the English speaking nations' common values from external and internal fantasies."[137] Brexit gives us the first opening to build the Anglosphere and tie Great Britain to the United States and move away from the bureaucratic European Union, which may be beginning its own implosion.

Who is part of the Anglosphere? Author James Bennett and Michael J. Lotus answer, *"Geographically, the densest nodes of the Anglosphere are found in the United States and Great Britain, while Anglosphere regions of Canada, Australia, New Zealand, Ireland, and South Africa are powerful and populous outliers. The educated English-speaking populations of the Caribbean, Oceania, Africa and India constitute the Anglosphere's frontiers."[138]*

Former Margaret Thatcher's advisor John O'Sullivan has called for an American policy that is pro-American while undermining the European Union super state. The present German government has is attempting to use the European Union as a tool for its own economic hegemony over Europe. Germany needs to tie Central

Europe to modern Europe and many Central Europeans want an American presence in Europe to safeguard their security, not just from the European Union dominated by Germany but a resurgent Russia to their east.

In the nations that form the Anglosphere, Bennett and Lotus note, "*The market economy is more than the absence of socialism. It is more than the absence of interventionist government; it is the economic expression of a strong civil society; just as substantive democracy is the political expression of a civil society and civic state.*" [139]While there is no rule that democracy and the market economy need to exist side by side, they often do. What matters is a civil society and understanding that government is but one player in society and part of a greater society. Religion, charities, and corporations of varied sizes as well as political parties are all players in society, and all interact with one another. A strong civil society sees individuals creating and working in a variety of enterprises, but the Left's attack on this civil society is threatening the foundations of our country.

For the Anglosphere nations, strong civic societies had their roots in medieval Europe. James C. Bennett and Michael Lotus contend that in the Middle Ages, particularly in England, the modern-day society was built upon mix of "tribal, feudal, local, church family and state institutions" [140] and the lack of a single overwhelming power capable of dominating. a nation. From the Magna Carta, English princes and barons made it clear to the crown that they had rights and this ideal became rooted in English custom and eventually made its way across the Atlantic. When civil society is strong, government can be limited to specific duties since welfare can be provided privately as well as publicly.

James C. Bennett and Michael Lotus do not yet consider India formally part of the Anglosphere but for the Anglosphere to dominate the 21st century, India must become part of the alliance.

They write, "*In such a commonwealth (Anglosphere), should the Indian choose to engage it, it may well be that Bangalore becomes a major center of the Anglosphere in thirty- or fifty-years' time. Anglospherists do not fear this, knowing that just as London is still great today because it shares an Anglosphere with New York and Los Angeles, it and the American metropolises will be great tomorrow partly because they might share it with Bangalore.*"[141]

Indian writer Gurcharan Das remembers attending Henry Kissinger's lectures at Harvard in the early 1960's and listening to Kissinger point out that Nehru was a dreamer and "it is dangerous to put dreamers in power." Kissinger's own views on Nehru may have been misplaced and he admitted it in his most recent book on diplomacy. Nehru was not an idealist and certainly not a pacifist like Gandhi. When force was needed, Nehru was prepared to use it. Four wars with Pakistan, including the liberation of Bangladesh from Pakistan in 1971, constant combat with China, and pushing the Portuguese out of Goa showed that India was not afraid of using military force. What Kissinger called a foreign policy of dreamers was a serious attempt to buy time for the new nation, residing as it does next to belligerent neighbors. Kissinger's own opinion from his Harvard days changed when he stated, "*India's conduct during the Cold War was not so different from that of the United States in its formative decades.*"[16] The difference is that in the United States' formative years, there was an ocean between America and Europe. India, on the other hand, is in a region populated by vipers and political rivals.

The United States, as the leader of NATO and the premier Western power, has inherited the traditional British interest in ensuring that no one single nation dominates the Eurasian landmass. India, also, has co-opted policy from its former English master. In 1934 Britain designed a plan to stabilize the Sino-Indian border and to dominate the Indian Ocean from Aden to Singapore.

India's present naval building effort reflects those same objectives. Like the United States, India does not want to see an Islamic fundamentalist revolution sweep through the Middle East. As China grows in strength and challenges the United States in the Far East, China also threatens India at her northern borders and through the sea-lanes including the Indian Ocean. India is crucial in both the development of alternatives to China's authoritarian state but also the expansion of the Anglosphere vision of the world. Trump made progress toward moving India toward our circle and the question is whether Biden's foreign policy team is smart enough to follow through this alliance or even understand its advantages

An America First policy should begin with the formation of the Anglosphere defense alliance, while adding additional allies against common foes. It also means to recognize what is in our national interest and what is not, to ensure that our resources are not wasted on nation-building but making sure we can project force when our national interest is at stake. America First is not isolationism, but a view that we *do* have our national interest. and we don't surrender our national identity and policy to transnational organizations. The Paris climate accord is an example of an agreement to avoid, as we would have put our economic and energy plans at the mercy of transnational organizations that would have reduced our ability to prosper. Even the supporters of the Paris Accord couldn't present evidence that it would reduce global warming. John Kerry views himself the master of the deal when it comes to climate change, but the Paris Accord is allowing China and India to delay their own efforts to reduce emissions while we are committed to doing it now.

If anything, the return of John Kerry to power demonstrates the failure of the leadership class. Kerry's career in the Senate was at best mediocre, He failed in his 2004 presidential bid, and his tenure as Secretary of State was part of the worst foreign policy team in the post-World II era. As the new climate czar, he will prove equally unequal to the task, as he has in the past.

A Republican foreign policy will put our foreign policy in our hands, instead of in the hands of transnational organizations, and will protect our national interest in a multipolar world.

Voter Fraud

I n a recent study, John R Lott, observed, "Vote fraud can increase voter turnout rate. Increased fraud can take many forms: higher rates of filling out absentee ballots for people who hadn't voted, dead people voting, ineligible people voting, or even payments to legally registered people for their votes. However, the increase might not be as large as the fraud if votes for opposing candidates are either lost, destroyed, or replaced with ballots filled out for the other candidate. The estimates here indicate that there were 70,000 to 79,000 "excess" votes in Georgia and Pennsylvania. Adding Arizona, Michigan, Nevada, and Wisconsin, the total increases to up to 289,000 excess votes." [142]

There are controversies over whether there was voter fraud in 2020 or whether the fraud committed did not exceed the margin of victory and Biden would still have won. Lott's own study noted that there may have been excess votes and as he noted, there are many ways to commit fraud. While Lott's data has been disputed, it does show that there were serious questions about the 2020 elections.

The New York 22nd congressional district demonstrated the chaos of the 2020 election. As National Review's John Fund told me, "With the various rules implemented in 2020 on a state level, it is hard to figure out when the incompetence ends and voting fraud begins." The rules are chaotic enough and the chaos of the New York 22nd district ended when Republican Claudia Tenney was then declared the winner. The reason for the chaos, John Fund noted, "How did this election count become such a meltdown? It started last year when New York Gov. Andrew Cuomo issued executive orders changing the state's election law in late August, with just over two months to go before Election Day... Without consulting the state Legislature, Cuomo added an unverified online portal for anyone to request an absentee ballot. It has since been taken down due to concerns over its complete lack of security...The watchdog group Judicial Watch says there is evidence that third-party groups may have used the portal to order ballots for individuals...Cuomo's order also added a requirement that defective absentee ballots could be "cured" by contacting the voters involved. This created huge burdens for local boards of elections and controversy over how each ballot was "cured" or not." [143]

As John Fund observed, "Safeguards against fraud that were dispensed with in many states during 2020 — such as having voters request and sign absentee ballot applications — must be restored. Signatures of voters on absentee ballots should be compared to the signature of the voters on their registration record before they are accepted." [144] The deadlines for absentee ballot in every state for completed Election Day itself and vote harvesting should be banned as allowing staffers and party activists to pick up ballots can intimidate voters according to John Fund. John Fund reminded me, "Both the U.S. Supreme Court and the bipartisan Commission on Federal Election Reform, co-chaired by former President Jimmy Carter and former Secretary of State James Baker, have found that fraud and errors by election officials can make the difference in a close election."

The proposed HR I For the People Act). would allow everything that John Fund believes should be forbidden and the result of what we saw in the New York 22nd district. In the Iowa 2nd district, Democrats in Congress thought about removing the duly elected

Marionette Miller-Meeks who was certified as the winner. While the margin was only six voters, her opponent could have appealed to Iowa state courts but instead she went straight to Congress and tried to have Nancy Pelosi simply bypass Iowa laws and remove Miller-Meeks from office. Republican opposition to this prevented Nancy Pelosi and her fellow Democrats from removing Rep. Miller-Meeks from her seat.

The Public Interest Legal Foundation noted what HR I, the Democrat efforts to ensure that future elections will feature the chaos of 2020 including:

- "Prohibits states from requiring more than a **signature to verify** a person's eligibility to register to vote. [Sec. 1004]
- Prohibits states from requiring **voter ID** at the polls- a sworn statement is all that can be required for identification. [Sec. 1903]
- Forces states to use **same-day registration**, requiring only signature attestation as to a registrant's eligibility, and requiring that the registrant be allowed to cast a vote that day, with no mention of it being provisional. [Sec. 1031]
- Prohibits states from banning **curbside voting** on Election Day. [Sec. 1908]
- Forces states to use **ballot drop boxes** for absentee and early voting and have them available at least 45 days before the election and "during all hours of the day." [Sec. 1907]
- **Automatically registers to vote** all eligible "individuals" (as opposed to "citizens") whose names and addresses appear in state and federal government databases (this also means that the federal government will decide a person's domicile and thus their taxing state). States have up to four months to even notify the person that they have been automatically registered. [Sec. 1012]

- Requires all "contributing" state and federal agencies, defined as those that possess a person's name, address, birthdate and citizen status, to send that information to the state election official for **automatic registration**. [Sec. 1014]
- Expands list of agencies that must offer **automatic voter registration** to those utilizing its services to include: state agencies that regulate gun sales (state Attorney General in most states), state departments of education, the Social Security Administration, the VA, the Defense Manpower Date Center of the Department of Defense, the Employee and Training Administration of the Department of Labor, the Center for Medicare and Medicaid Services, the Bureau of Citizenship and Immigration, and the Federal Bureau of Prisons, which must automatically register a convicted felon to vote so long as the felon has completed "any part of" of his sentence. [Sec. 1013(e)]

Prohibits contributing agencies that do not ask for **citizenship status** in their normal course of business from completing any service transactions for the person until he or she either registers to vote or declines to register to vote (previously such agencies were just required to offer a registration form). [Sec. 1013(c)(2)]" [145]

This law will allow all the controversial methods used in the 2020 election, like curbside voting, increased mail-in ballots while allowing party activists to pick up ballots and all of which will increase voting fraud or make it difficult if not impossible to find it. Not asking for citizens for their citizenship status HOW? ID? will allow an increase no citizens voting. Americas Majority Foundation reviewed non-citizens voting in key battleground states and national polls over three elections cycle 2014, 2016 and 2018.

There is certainly enough evidence to show that a significant number of non-citizens are voting across the United States. Jesse Richman and David Earnest of Old Dominion University reviewed incidents of voting by non-citizens, and while some have argued that illegal voting is inconsequential, Richman and Earnest attempted to find exactly how many non-citizens voted. They concluded that, "Most non-citizens do not register, let alone vote. But enough do that their participation can change the outcome of close races." [146]

Using data from the Cooperative Congressional Election Study, they attempted to find out how many non-citizens voted. They found that 14% of non-citizens in both the 2008 and 2010 samples were registered to vote. From that they estimated that 6.5% of non-citizens voted in 2008 and 2.2% voted in 2010. Their estimation was based on CCES samples that Obama won 80% of non-citizens' votes and while this did not affect the general election, they speculated that it could have accounted for some Democratic victories in Senate races. Those races include Al Franken's victory over Norm Coleman in 2008. Franken's margin was 312 votes and as they concluded, "Votes cast by just 65 percent of Minnesota non-citizens could account for this margin. It is also possible that noncitizen votes were responsible for Obama's 14,177 votes, so a turnout by 5.1% of North Carolina adult non-citizens would have provided the margin for Obama's victory in North Carolina." [147]

Richman and Earnest believe that it was entirely possible that the Electoral College votes of North Carolina could have been switched from McCain to Obama by illegal voters. While the fate of North Carolina didn't matter on the overall election results in 2008, in a closer election it could matter. In both 2016 and 2020, the election was decided by less than 100,000 votes in several swing states.

Richman and Earnest noted that three quarters of non-citizen had photo ID's when asked to provide them, making it easier
for them to vote. Virginia Republican activist William Campenni,
writing in Power Line, observed, "For years here in Virginia I
have observed massive fraud – in the registration process, in the
absentee ballot casting, in the battle to remove photo IDs, in the
voting at the polls. Recent studies have shown thousands of illegal
alien registrations in Virginia, and hundreds of voters also casting
votes in other states (college kids the worst offenders). My own
identity (SS No.) was stolen last year and used to get a fraudulent tax refund and voting... For over a decade the SEIU and its
local affiliates have gone through the extensive illegal alien community here in Virginia fraudulently registering illegals who then
vote in large numbers, usually in early voting or absentee ballots,
because there are no poll watchers to challenge them. They even
brag about it." [148]

Campenni added that the incumbent Republican, Sen. George
Allen, may have lost to Jim Webb in Virginia in 2006 because of
illegal voters and Governor Terry McAuliffe may have won his
seat in 2013 owing their participation. He concluded, "(Mark)
Warner defeated Ed Gillespie for Senate in 2014 by the small vote
differences provided by illegals. And my friend the local former
Fairfax County Democrat head brags about it when we have coffee
together." [149]

J. Christian Adams, an election lawyer who served in the voting
rights section at the U.S. Department of Justice under President
George W. Bush mentioned the result of a study conducted by the
Public Interest Legal Foundation that looked into a small number
of Virginia counties and found that 1000 were removed from the
rolls due to citizenship problems. At least 200 of these individuals
voted. Democratic operative John Podesta in emails disclosed by
WikiLeaks: "Podesta seems to have figured out that, because of

vulnerabilities in our election system, foreigners can get registered to vote and get voter ID at the same time. Podesta's right, and has revealed one the biggest vulnerabilities in American elections, all because of the Motor Voter law." [150]

The Public Interest Legal Foundation followed up on this study and found even more discrepancies as they reviewed 133 Virginia jurisdictions. They found that between 2011 and May of 2017, Virginia removed 5500 illegal voters and found that over 1800 of these individuals had cast nearly 7500 ballots. As Richman and Earnest noted, 80% of non-citizens voted for Obama in 2008 and a Pew Research Center survey estimated that those non-citizens who identify with a political party do so at a three to one ratio in favor of Democrats.

The Government Accountability Institute studied duplicate voters from registration and found significant fraud. As Hans A. von Spakovsky noted, "The Government Accountability Institute was able to obtain voter registration and voter history data from only 21 states because while some states shared it freely, 'others impose exorbitant costs or refuse to comply with voter information requests'...The institute compared the lists using an "extremely conservative matching approach that sought only to identify two votes cast in the same legal name." It found that 8,471 votes in 2016 were "highly likely" duplicates...Extrapolating this to all 50 states would likely produce, with "high-confidence," around 45,000 duplicate votes."[151] These data may be the tip of the voter fraud iceberg.

In two national polls we conducted after the 2018 elections, we found evidence of non-citizens voting in big number. In the Cygnal poll, 0.7% of voters reported they were no-citizens but 0.3% were not sure if they were citizens. In the Voice Broadcasting poll, 0 6% of the voters admitted they were non-citizens and 0.3% were not sure if they were citizens. Overall, when combining the individual states and two national polls, we found that 0.4% of voters admitted that they were not citizens and another 0.2% admitted they were not sure about their citizenship. At a 0.4% rate, we are looking at as many as 450,000 non-citizens voting in the 2018 election.

Overall, we have surveyed a little over 90,000 voters from the end of the 2016 elections. Our pollsters asked voters if they were citizens and 1.65% of voters admitted that they were not legal citizens. This could translate out to over 2,300,000 illegal voters in the 2020 election. Our research along with others show that general election, illegal voters are nearly three times more likely to vote in the general election. Even at the lower range we in our 2018 post-election, our research showed that the number of illegal voters could range between 300,000 to 2,400,000 voters based on our numbers.

That is a widespread across the country, and we are talking an average of 6,000 illegal voters per state to 50,000 per state. While we did not research Florida or Arizona, we can surmise the possibility that illegal voters could have affected the Florida Senate race, which was close enough to be in the margin of fraud. If we go conservative and follow the trend of many of the states, we looked at in 2018, at .02%, we are talking a possibility of 16,000 illegal voters in a Senate raced decided by around 10,000 votes in Republican Rick Scott's favor. In 2020, the numbers of overall voters were higher, and the question is. "Was this presidential election decided by fraud"? This is certainly possible, and if past research holds true, the number of illegal voters nearly triple in presidential elections. and who knows how many illegal non-citizens participated in the 2020 election. While the number of illegal non-citizen voters overlooked in this election, it will once again be a possible factor in 2022 and beyond.

In the Public Interest Legal Foundation study, the researchers found Virginia quietly removed illegal voters from the voter roll in selected counties and that a third of them actually voted an average of 3 to 4 elections before being removed. In our study, we found that 83% of illegal voters who admitted voting in multiple elections, reinforcing that illegal voter don't just vote but they are voting in multiple elections while on the voting roll. Rich Lowry in *National Review* noted, "Although usually not as extensive or consequential as what may have transpired in North Carolina's 9th District, vote fraud often involves absentee voting, and exploiting poor and vulnerable voters. In October, four people were indicted in Texas on 30 felony counts of targeting elderly voters in a fraudulent mail-in voter scheme…Rules should be rigorous, and it's insane that the sort of vote harvesting that (McCrae) Dowless engaged in — i.e., a private party collecting the ballots of voters — is perfectly legal in California." [152]

Mark Harris was a Republican, who won his congressional election by a close margin, but the election was not certified due to allegation of voter fraud and a special election was called in 2019. In ballot harvesting, paper absentee ballots are collected by intermediaries who are supposed to deliver them polling officials. In Real Clear Investigations, Government Accountability Institute research director Eric Eggers noted, "The latter is suspected in North Carolina, where uncharacteristic Democratic charges of vote fraud prompted an investigation into whether Republican-paid political operatives illegally collected and possibly stole absentee ballots in a still-undecided congressional race. A national spotlight was shone by the *New York Times*, which, like Democrats, often minimizes vote fraud; it flooded the zone in this case, assigning five reporters to a single story…In California, by contrast, Democrats exulted as they credited a quietly passed 2016 law legalizing ballot-harvesting with their recent sweep of House seats in the former Republican stronghold of Orange County, thereby helping them win control of the House. In that case, it was Republican eyebrows that were arched. House Speaker Paul Ryan said what happened in California "defies logic.""[153]

What happened in North Carolina could easily have happened in California, but the difference is that no one in the media or in the Democratic-controlled secretary of state's office in California are anxious to see if what appeared to happen in North Carolina could have happened in California. While we found that number of illegal voters based on our research of one California district did not impact the election in 2018, ballot harvesting is ripe for massive voter fraud. Combine easier access to paper ballots by unscrupulous political operatives and illegal voters allowed to stay on the voters' roll and you have a recipe for massive voter fraud.

While there is much handwringing about "voter suppression" in the state of Georgia in 2018, Gov. Brian Kemp proved very inept at voter suppression if that was his goal. As the Secretary of State in Georgia, which has strict voter ID requirements, Haris Alic and Jeffrey Cimmino noted, "In 2018, the turnout totals rivaled prior presidential election years. In 2016, more than 59 percent of registered voters—or about 4 million—cast a ballot in Georgia, with similar numbers in 2012…Abrams was a prime beneficiary of this surge in turnout, capturing more votes than any Democrat running statewide since 2008. Her 1.9 million vote total exceeded Hillary Clinton's 2016 performance by 34,000 votes and outpaced the Democratic Party's 2014 nominee for governor by 800,000 votes…Demographic-based turnout data are not yet available from the Georgia secretary of state's office, but exit polls indicate African-American turnout was comparable to previous years." [154]His opponent, Stacey Abrams, nearly won, and her votes were impressive and yet she complained about "voter suppression."

But as Alic and Cimmino noted, any problems with voters put in a pending category lays on her and her campaign's shoulders when they wrote, "The *Wall Street Journal* observed that Abrams, herself, may hold some responsibility for the significant number of voters labeled with a "pending" status prior to the election… The [exact match] law was intended to prevent groups from sloppily filling out applications for individuals, as Ms. Abrams's New Georgia Project appears to have done," the paper's editorial board wrote…Benita Dodd, vice president of the Georgia Public Policy Foundation, told the *Washington Free Beacon* a large number of "pending votes" were the result of "outside groups signing up people to vote using paper registration forms" instead of urging them to register online." [155]

There are two lessons to draw from the Georgia experience in 2018. Democrats want looser elections laws and have proved to be obstacles to any efforts to ensure fairer elections. Laws such as voter ID's will not suppress votes, as voter turnout—including minority turnout—has increased in Georgia despite tougher voter ID laws has increased include minority participation. The real question to opponents who consistently reject any efforts to ensure that those who are ineligible to vote can't vote is to ask, "Why *should* people who are ineligible to vote be able to vote? Conservatives, when approaching this issue, should use the language of civil rights and the need for confidence in elected institutions. But in 2020, Georgia once again became one of the key areas and much of the issues we saw nationwide existed and all the lessons we should have learned from 2018, were not learned.

In Georgia, the Republican Secretary of State entered a compromised settlement to change the statutory requirements for reviewing signatures on absentee ballots to confirm the voter's identity. This made it more difficult to challenge voters. This surrender led to the Georgia disaster where both Senate seats flipped to the Democrats. In March of 2021, Georgia strengthened their election laws to include more strengthen Voter ID provision for absentee ballots.

Conclusion

History is but a fickle thing, based on the interpretation of historians who, like many within the academic class, do not always get it right. The period of 2020-2021 is like the period of 1918-1921, when the United States was burdened by a severe pandemic. Nearly 700,000 Americans died of the Spanish flu, equal to about 2,000,000 Americans today. At the same time, and the federal government economic policies were paralyzed by Woodrow Wilson's stroke, which incapacitated him. A small circle surrounding him, including his wife, Edith, ran the government. Not even Vice President Thomas Marshall was fully aware of Wilson's illness. With a pandemic raging, the economic policies were disastrous as soldiers returned home to an economic slipping into depression. The Wilson Administration still had the wartime economy in place, with high tax rates, the Federal Reserve pumping out money and much of the wartime controls of industries by the state still in place. The boards the Wilson administration created during the war to control all aspects of production laid the groundwork for the New Deal and have become part of the inspiration for the Green New Deal.

The economy after World War I slipped into an inflationary spiral like the inflation that ravaged America in the late 1970's and early 1980's and unemployment went to the double-digits. The Great Depression of the 1930's nearly happened in 1920-21.

Warren Harding proved to be the right president for the times. A modest man, he put together a strong cabinet. In *National Review*, Kyle Smith wrote, "America in 1921 was in a state of crisis, reeling from the worst recession in half a century, the most severe deflationary spiral on record, and the 1918 Spanish flu pandemic, which killed 675,000 people in a nation of a little more than 100 million. Unemployment, it is now estimated, stood somewhere between 8.7 and 11.7 percent as returning soldiers inflated the size of the working-age population. Between 1919 and August of 1921 the Dow Jones average plummeted 47 percent…Harding's response to this emergency was largely to let the cycle play out. It was, James Grant wrote in *The Forgotten Depression*, 'the last governmentally unmediated business cycle downturn.' The recession ended in mid-year1, and boom times followed. Harding and Congress cut federal spending nearly in half, from 6.5 percent of GDP to 3.5 percent. The top tax rate came down from 73 percent to 25, and the tax base broadened. Unemployment came down to an estimated 2 to 4 percent." [156]

Harding succeeded in taming inflation and got the economy going strong, and the Roaring Twenties continued even after his death in 1923. Smith continued, "White racism, in part motivated by the recent return of newly empowered black soldiers from the European theater, was at a high-water mark. The Ku Klux Klan, reborn during the Woodrow Wilson years, was flourishing, having received a mammoth boost from the blockbuster film *The Birth of a Nation*, which Wilson famously screened at the White House, and which contained a quotation from Wilson's best-known book, *A History of the American People*, praising the 'great Ku Klux Klan.' Wilson had also resegregated the military and the federal workforce." [157]Harding's family were Ohio abolitionists, this self-made man made a plea for civil rights of Blacks when he accepted his party's nomination in 1920. He stated, "I believe the Negro citizens of America should be guaranteed the enjoyment of all their rights, that they have earned their full measure of citizenship bestowed, that their sacrifices in blood on the battlefields of the republic have entitled them to all of freedom and opportunity, all of sympathy and aid that the American spirit of fairness and justice demands."

Harding supported anti-lynching laws, made a speech in the Deep South passionately calling for civil rights for Blacks and he reversed much of Wilson's illiberal moves, freeing socialist Eugene Debs and other opponents of Wilson and World War I from prison. Wilson, after all, was racist, viewed the Constitution that he was elected to uphold with disdain and during the War, enacted laws that sent antiwar activists to prison.

Harding inherited a precarious situation that could have spun out of control and the revolting authoritarianism in place by Wilson could have been locked in place, if Debs and others sent to prison for their speech stayed locked in jail. Yet even the great progressive judge Oliver Wendell Holmes viewed anti-war leaflets as "shouting fire in a crowded theater" and argued that the authors of these leaflets should be jailed.

Harding succeeded in stirring the American ship back and he restored a classically liberal, rights-focused, limited government and the roaring 20's happened only to end by progressive policies engineered by Hoover and a recovery delayed by FDR's New Deal. Historian Paul Johnson concluded about Harding and the 1920's, "the treatment of Harding is worth dwelling on because, taken in conjunction with a similar denigration of his vice-president and successor Calvin Coolidge, a man of totally different temperament, it amounts to the systematic misrepresentation of public policy over a whole era." [158]

The lessons of the Harding administration are a lesson for conservatives moving forward. Kyle Smith noted one important lesson, "One hundred years ago this month, one of our greatest presidents took office. In a moment of national crisis, Warren G. Harding restored the economic health of the United States. Harding was also, for a man of his time, atypically enlightened about the perniciousness of racism, and, contrary to legend, honest. That none of this is generally acknowledged is due to a posthumous series of smears by left-wing journalists and historians, which started with a hatchet job in *The New Republic.* Harding's legacy is perhaps modern America's first example of how an ideologically motivated media and academic establishment can set about dismantling politically inconvenient truths and installing a false narrative in their place." [159]

The modern left is attempting to rewrite our history, just as they rewrote the history about Harding and Coolidge era, with publications such as "the 1619 Project," in which they portray our country as a land conceived in racism and slavery, an experiment no longer worthy of support. They also support Critical Race Theory, which argues that racism is so entrenched in our society and must be rooted out by any means necessary OK? But the reality is that Critical Race Theory *is* racist, presenting itself as a world in which America is permanently separated by gender and race, and all attempts at critiquing the theory explained as "white fragility" with some races given more attention through government. In Oakland, an experiment in basic guaranteed income is going on in which the poorest will be given a monthly stipend, but poor white families are excluded from the program because of their race. Asian Americans are being openly discriminated at universities in favor of other minorities as our society moves toward a society based on a new society controlled by oligarchies, with prizes handed out to the races favored by the party in power. The dream of a color-blind America in which a person's worth is judged by the content of their character is disappearing and it is the socialists who are leading the charge against a color-blind society.

Race has become the central theme of our society, while those at the bottom and in the middle who belong to non-favored races are seeing their dreams short-circuited.

In 2020, America was at its worst and its best. At its worst, we had governors who like Woodrow Wilson did, abandoned basic liberties as businesses were declared "non-essential" and closed to stop an infection. Fines were handed out to those who disobeyed dared to reopen, such as in Texas when a young woman who ran her own salon was hauled before a court. When a judge told her, she was being selfish for opening her business, her response should ring out across America, when she told the judge it is not selfish for her to take care of her family and keep her business open so her employees could provide for their families.

The irony for a moment in history, America had its Warren Harding moment. Starting in May 2020, President Trump campaigned to reopen the economy and a few brave governors did exactly that. America alternated between government stimulus and productive capitalism in which capitalism was winning out as 2020 ended. From April 2020 going into March 2021, the unemployment dropped from 14.4 percent to 6 percent as those governors who opened their states led the way in increasing employment. Non-lockdown states and red states led the way toward recovery. More jobs were created in the last seven months of the Trump administration in a recovery from the covid-19 recession. By contrast, it that it took five years for Obama/Biden economic policies to create enough jobs to recover from the Great Recession. The American economy was strong in February of 2020, so the recovery was built on a was a strong economy when the government chose to close the economy for what was supposed to 15 days to slow the virus to give states a chance not to be overwhelmed by the virus. But in many states the lockdowns remained in force for the rest of the year. The states with the most restrictive economies did not see any overall benefit when it came to saving lives, but they did manage to increase economic distress among their citizens, with Main Street, the middle class and blue collar workers who couldn't work from home (including blue-collar minorities) the hardest hit.

What we need now is a Warren Harding, but we ended up with Joe Biden, who has all the worst qualities of Wilson without any of his intellectual firepower, and at his best, Biden showed himself as mediocre over a half of century political career. Biden wants massive government at a time when leaner government is required. The Federal Reserve today is increasing the money supply to keep the economy from collapsing while we are expanding stimulus with $2 trillion in the first round and trillions more on the way. in spending 90 percent of which has as the Administration opening proposals with more to come, ninety percent had nothing to do with Covid relief and much of it subsidizing those states who chose to restrict their economies and thus increase their unemployment. There will be three trillion dollars stimulus for "rebuilding infrastructure." Most of which has nothing to do with repairing roads and bridges. Of course, these gigantic programs will be paid for by taxing the rich and raising corporate taxes in the name of "equity." What is missing is any plan to increase productivity and economic growth. Depending on government spending to produce growth is a recipe for disaster.

The left, through their allies in Big Tech, are working on censoring their opponents. Civil liberties are at risk just as they were during the Wilson Administration. While the left pretends to fight racism, their emphasis on race is in fact racist as different groups will be treated differently and not equally under the law. Just as Wilson viewed the Constitution with disdain, so does the left today work on creating their own tyranny of the majority with no real protection for minority rights.

The real beginning of resistance against this modern threat begins with the States. There are 27 Republican governors, and they have control of half of the state legislatures. The first order of business is that states should be allowed to determine control over voting, including ensuring that only legal citizens vote. Ron DeSantis has shown how to resist the Federal machine when he didn't depend upon the scientific class for advice but relied on those whose were outside of the politicized scientific class and who proved to be correct in their analysis. He worked on protecting the most vulnerable and rebuilt his economy after the initial shock in April and May of 2020.

Republicans are now the party of the working class and looking at what ideas can benefit the working class. Trump understood this in 2015 when others didn't and his administration did raise the income of those in the middle class, the lower class and minorities. It was the economic restrictions during the pandemic that hurt the middle class, lower class and minorities, and leftist Democrat governors like Andrew Cuomo and Gavin Newsom instituted most of those restrictions. Throughout the pandemic, New York and California unemployment were significantly higher than the national average throughout 2020 and entering 2021.

American Enterprise Institute fellow Ramesh Ponnuru observed, "At the same time, Republicans have been declaring a new self-understanding. On Election Night, Hawley tweeted, 'We are a working-class party now.' A few days later, Rubio was only a little more cautious: 'The future of the party is based on a multiethnic, multiracial working-class coalition'" Representative Jim Jordan (R., Ohio) has joined the chorus. The GOP, he said, "is no longer the 'wine and cheese' party. It's the beer and blue jeans party.'" [160]

Ponnuru points out the difficulty of designing a platform to take advantage of this new coalition, "One reason that consensus on a policy agenda for the working class may be elusive is that the definition of the group itself is ambiguous. Look at the relationship between voting behavior and income, and the notion that the Republicans are becoming a working-class party looks illusory. AP Votecast found that about 40 percent of the 2020 electorate belonged to households making less than $50,000 a year, and Joe Biden got most of their votes. Trump did best among voters making between $50,000 and $100,000. One could reasonably consider those voters in the core of the middle class. The Census reports that in 2019, median income was $69,000: Half of households made more, and half less… These days, when people talk about how the working-class votes, they are generally referring to levels of schooling rather than of income. As recently as 2012, college graduates were a bit more likely to vote Republican than everyone else. In 2020, those with college degrees were significantly more likely than others to vote Democratic. (That excludes voters with postgraduate degrees, who have long given a majority of their votes to Democrats.) This education-based realignment has occurred throughout the developed world and has taken the same basic form, with voters who have college degrees to the left of those without." [161]

In two separate elections, Trump received 47% of the vote and while you can argue that the pandemic hurt his chances to win in 2020, there is the fact that the Democrats went from 45 percent to 51 percent from 2016 to 2020 in the suburbs, which means that Democrats increased their support among suburban voters by 6 to 9 million, wiping out the advantages Trump gain from 1.5 to 2 million votes gained from minority voters. White voters in the suburbs carried Joe Biden over the top. But was this switch due to Trump's personality or a more lasting change? Ramesh Ponnuru noted, "Assuming Republicans can figure out how to build on their recent working-class success, they will have to decide how avidly to court another group: the college-educated white voters who have been dumping them. Some of them found Trump repulsive but will remember what they liked about Republicans if he does not continue to loom so large in the party. In some places, Republican candidates will make winning back these voters a priority. In most places and in the long run, though, Republicans will probably find it more important to court their new working-class constituency."[162]

Over the past two elections, Michigan, Pennsylvania and, Wisconsin looked more purple than total blue as Republicans and Democrats split these two states. But Republicans are finding that Georgia and Arizona have joined the ranks of purple states, states that were once dependably red. Eventually, the Republicans will have to regain Georgia and Arizona while turning Michigan, Pennsylvania, and Wisconsin red permanently. Republicans also need to find other blue states to turn into competitive purple ones. Presently it would be difficult to see California or New York any-time soon turning purple, but Illinois might be the right target. In 2014, the GOP took the governor race along with two con-gressional seats, and Democratic Sen. Dick Durbin got only 53 percent of the vote against a weak candidate. In the governor's race, Republican Bruce Rauner lost Cook County by only 350,000 votes but got 500,000 more votes. He took all but one county in the state. Republicans took advantage of a multiethnic, multiracial working class as Rauner and Jim Oberweis in 2014 both exceeded previous Republicans' performance among Hispanics. (Oberweis did lose but did far better than expected and Durbin was nervous about his prospects.) The Trump Coalition existed in 2014, even before it was called the Trump Coalition and there were "Trump Republicans."

The Democrats are now the socialist party of America and are attempting to find their majority-minority coalition with subur-banites, public sector union members, minorities and the very wealthy who are the chief funders of this coalition. Republicans have yet to decide what party they are, but fate is already deciding for them. Big Business and the very wealthy are now funding the Democrat Party, seeing that they can take advantage of the corporatist policies emanating from Washington to enrich themselves and shut down their opponents. The Democrats will be a vehicle to pursue the leftist agenda, including the Green New Deal from green cars to wind and solar energy. We will see an alliance of Big Tech, Wall Street, the administrative state and socialists within the political class controlling all aspects of our lives while those at the top enrich themselves. Joel Kotkin has called this agenda "the new feudalism" and when this is combined with attempts to censor their opponents, , we may be seeing the formation of a **Feudal Fascism** with government directing companies to produce what the government wants while workers will simply be cogs in the machine.

Republicans are left with the task of combining an agenda that benefits the middle class and allows the poor the ability to climb the economic ladder, while defending the free market economy. We must also deal with a culture war that is far larger than culture wars in the past. It is not just about abortion even though abortion matters but goes beyond that. Parents will find their daughters competing against "transgender" boys and be called bigots if they want girls to only compete against girls in athletic competition. It is about defending those basic principles that bring success, like showing up to work on time, don't work while stoned, do the best you can in school and wait until you are married before you have children. These were values that three decades ago wouldn't even be debatable but today but advocating them now marks you as supporting "white privilege." *We are living in a land where the cultural norm will be mediocrity as opposed to meritocracy*

Trump's future may not be as a candidate but as defender of his populist worldview. Trump has talked of starting his own social media company to challenge Facebook and Twitter and this could be a challenge to the Big Tech monopoly. As Claremont *Review of Books* editor Charles Kesler noted, Trump brings out his supporters, but he also brings out his opponents' voters. The good news is that Republican and conservatives have a deep bench for 2024, beginning with Marco Rubio and Josh Hawley who are attempting to find solutions from the Senate. While Kristi Noem may have stubbed her toe on the transgender issue in not signing a bill that forbids men from competing with women in high school sports, she still has plenty of time to figure out a way to recover from this mistake. Her ability to steer her state through the pandemic was admirable and like Ron DeSantis, she took her share of abuse. DeSantis has shown how to get through a crisis and move his state forward with solutions that worked. There are others out there ready to lead.

The Republicans and the conservatives within the Party must do more than just oppose the Democrats. They need to present an agenda that will give Americans a fair opportunity to succeed and preserve the American Dream.

Final Notes

This book is the beginning of a series of essays and books that will follow up on what is happening in America and pursue the path we need to follow. The lessons of this book and writings that follow will be based on the following premises:

1. Our leadership class is totally broken and beyond repair, and it is time to replace this class with a new class ready to lead. Our leadership class is feckless and no longer committed what is good for our society but is primarily concerned with pursuing their own gains whether it is the political class continuing to gain power to Washington, the scientific class has been corrupted by politics and view themselves like a conclave of cardinals. They view themselves as the defender of knowledge, and already know the answers to questions that still elude us.

2. Our media class has become the propaganda wing of the political and scientific class,

3. Our academic class, like the scientific class, no longer seeks truth but simply indoctrinate their students in their version of truth. In 2020, the academic and scientific class ceased to search for truth. The pursuit of truth is no longer the goal of our scientific and academic class. The goals of these classes are to punish those who still seek truth.

4. Our business class, like much of the leadership class, no longer believes in the very system that has enriched them and now seeking resetting the system to benefit them but pull the ladder out from those entrepreneurs coming up behind them. They want to freeze our progress where it is today, no longer innovating but making sure tomorrow's innovators below never see their dreams come true.

The Democratic Party is completely broken as an institution, incapable of governing or defending the values that made this country great. It is a socialist party running closer to the Chinese model of national socialism in which the government allots economic prosperity, and the masses are mere clogs in the economic machine frozen in their status. As Joel Kotkin and others are fearing, we are headed toward a feudal fascist state, and it is the democratic socialists within the Democratic Party that are leading us there.

Over the past few years, I have looked back to history to see how best tie Trump populism to a Reagan free market approach, to move away from victimhood to an idea that America is still a great country that will give all a fair opportunity to succeed. The average American loves the entrepreneurs who put their own life and soul into their company, but they hate those who run major corporations who manage the companies for they view those leaders with no skin in the game.

Apple is no longer the Apple of Steven Jobs and Microsoft is no longer the Microsoft of the younger Bill Gates. The older Bill Gates is now running his foundation and looking for ways to reset capitalism and save us from "a warming planet" but destroying the very society that produced his wealth to begin with. Maybe Bill Gates wants us to eat fake meat, but most Americans still love a ribeye. The tech oligarchies are colluding with much of the left wing of the political class (and the left dominates much of the political class) to protect their present place in society while destroying their competition and censoring those ideas that challenge the status quo.

When Republicans turn toward a national theme of defending the culture and the American dream, they triumph. The Democratic Party no longer believes individuals should be judged by the content of their characters but judged by the color of their skin with some races rated higher than others. The democratic socialist movement is becoming the racist movement of our society and the defender of a caste system in which they remain at the top of the heap.

The good news in such dark times is that there is a leadership class ready to challenge the old order and move this country forward. The past year showed that there are new leaders out in the hinterland just as Ron DeSantis who has shown how to lead in difficult times. The new leadership classes are now outside of Washington and the new leaders living outside of Washington can lead us away from the concentration of government in Washington toward a new dispersion of power toward a more local approach that will benefit us all.

The journey begins.

Acknowledgements

I want to thank the following people including Wilfred Reilly, Jim Echols, JD Johannes, and Clara Del Villar for their ideas, and research contributions. I also want to thank Martin Wooster for editing and advice on this book.

I also want to acknowledge my family including my wife for patience as I wrote this book.

Enjoy this book and understand all is not lost.

Endnotes

1   Sean Illing, "The Intellectual Case For Trump: A Debate," Vox, March 23, 2021, https://www.vox.com/policy-and-politics/22278065/donald-trump-conservative-politics-charles-kesler (accessed April 15, 2021)

2   Glenn Harlan Reynolds, "The Suicide of Expertise," *USA Today*, March 20, 2017, https://www.usatoday.com/story/opinion/2017/03/20/americans-reject-experts-failure-history-glenn-reynolds-column/99381952/ (accessed April 16, 2021)

3   Glenn Harlan Reynolds, "The suicide of Expertise," *USA Today*, March 20, 2017, https://www.usatoday.com/story/opinion/2017/03/20/americans-reject-experts-failure-history-glenn-reynolds-column/99381952/ (accessed April 16, 2021)

4   Tweet from "Wretchard The Cat," February 17, 2017, https://twitter.com/wretchardthecat/status/832732563722498049 (accessed April 16, 2021)

5   Glenn Harlan Reynolds, "Trump And The Crisis of The Meritocracy," *USA Today*, February 20, 2017, https://www.usatoday.com/story/opinion/2017/02/20/trump-elite-brexit-rome-crisis-glenn-reynolds-column/98132442/ (accessed April 16, 2021)

6   Glenn Harlan Reynolds, "Trump and The Crisis of The Meritocracy," USA Today, February 20, 2017, https://www.usatoday.com/story/opinion/2017/02/20/trump-elite-brexit-rome-crisis-glenn-reynolds-column/98132442/ (accessed April 16, 2021) (italics added)

7   Joel Kotkin, "Can The GOP Fatten Itself Up Around The Middle?" *Riverside Press-Enterprise*, December 13, 2015, https://www.pe.com/2015/12/13/joel-kotkin-can-gop-fatten-up-around-the-middle/ (accessed April 16, 2021)

8   Tom Donelson, *The Rise of National Populism and Democratic Socialism* (New York: Post Hill Press, 2017)

9   Glenn H. Reynolds, "GameStop Insurgency Is Just The Latest Rebellion Against "The Big Guys," *New York Post*, January 28, 2021, https://nypost.com/2021/01/28/gamestop-insurgency-just-latest-rebellion-against-the-big-guys/ (accessed April 16, 2021)

10   Wilfred Reilly with F. Jane Lingle, *An Ignored Cost The Effect of Yes-No Lockdown Strategy, Along With Red-Blue Political Partisanship and Other Variables, On April-August Unemployment Across U.S. States* (Marion, Iowa: Americas Majority Foundation, 2020), 10-11.

11   Carrie Sheffield, "A Tale of Two Covid Economies: Red State Recovery, Blue State Recession," Just The News, October 15, 2020, https://justthenews.com/nation/economy/tale-two-recoveries-red-states-outpacing-blue-states-economic-growth-driven (accessed April29, 2021):

12   Dan McLaughlin, "Unemployment in Red and Blue States," National Review Online, April 22, 2021 https://www.nationalreview.com/corner/unemployment-in-red-and-blue-states/ (accessed April 29, 2021)

13   "'Lockdown Is A Terrible Experiment,'" Spiked, October 9, 2020, https://www.spiked-online.com/2020/10/09/lockdown-is-a-terrible-experiment/ (accessed April 30, 2021) (italics added)

14   Wilfred Reilly, *Reviewing The Data On The Efficacy Of The Lockdown And Comparison of Red States Versus Blue States Dealing With Covid-19* (Marion, Iowa: Americas Majority Foundation, 2020), 4-6.

15   Wilfred Reilly with F. Jane Lingle, *An Ignored Cost: The Effect of Yes-No Lockdown Strategy, Along With Red-Blue Political Partisanship And Other Variables, On April-August Unemployment Rates* (Marion, Iowa: Americas Majority Foundation, 2020), 4-6.

16 Dhaval M. Dave, Joseph J. Sain, and Samuel Safford, Statewide *Opening During Mass Vaccination: Evidence on Mobility, Public Health, and Economic Activity From Texas*, National Bureau of Economic Research, May 2021, https://www.nber.org/system/files/working_papers/w28804/w28804.pdf (accessed May 25, 2021)

17 "Great Barrington Declaration," https://gbdeclaration.org/#read (accessed April 27, 2021).

18 Casey B. Mulligan, *Economic Activity And The Value of Medical Innovation During A Pandemic*, National Bureau Of Economic Research Working Paper 27060, 2 https://www.nber.org/system/files/working_papers/w27060/w27060.pdf (accessed April 30, 2021)

19 Sergio Correia, Stephen Luck, and Emil Vermer, "Forget The Pandemic, Save The Economy: Lessons From The 1918 Flu Pandemic," Federal Reserve Bank of New York, March 27, 2020, https://libertystreeteconomics.newyorkfed.org/2020/03/fight-the-pandemic-save-the-economy-lessons-from-the-1918-flu.html (accessed April 30, 2021)

20 Lee H. Ohanian, "What—Or Who—Started The Great Depression," National Bureau of Economic Research Working Paper 15258, 52, https://www.nber.org/papers/w15258 (accessed August 7, 2021)

21 Harold B. Cole and Lee H. Ohanian, *New Deal Policies and The Persistence Of The Great Depression: A General Equilibrium Analysis* (Federal Reserve Bank of Minneapolis, Research Department, Working Paper 597), 1.

22 Donald J. Boudreaux and Alberto Mingardi, "The Economy Is Not A Machine," *City Journal*, April 22, 2020, https://www.city-journal.org/covid-19-market-process-revival (accessed April 30, 2021)

23 Donald J. Boudreaux and Alberto Mingardi, "The Economy Is Not A Machine," *City Journal*, April 27, 2020, https://www.city-journal.org/covid-19-market-process-revival (accessed April 30, 2021)

24 Tom Donelson, *The Rise of National Populism and Democratic Socialism* (New York: Post Hill Press, 2017)

25 Tom Donelson, *The Rise of national Populism and Democratic Socialism* (New York: Post Hill Press, 2017)

26 Tom Donelson, *The Rise of national Populism and Democratic Socialism* (New York: Post Hill Press, 2017)

27 Donald J. Boudreaux and Alberto Mingardi, "The Economy Is Not a Machine, " *City Journal*, April 27, 2020, https://www.city-journal.org/covid-19-market-process-revival (accessed April 30, 2021) (italics added)

28 Matt Ridley, "Britain Is In Danger Of Repeating Its Post-War Mistakes,"art9icle from *The Spectator* posted on Matt Ridley Online, April 17, 2021, https://www.mattridley.co.uk/blog/repeating-post-war-mistakes/ (accessed August 7, 2021)

29 Tom Donelson, Clara Del Villar, and JD Johannes, The Pursuit of Economic Growth (Marion, Iowa: Americas Majority Foundation, 2020)

30 Tyler Clifford, "Jim Cramer: The Pandemic Led To 'One Of The Greatest Wealth Transfers In History," cnbc.com, June 4, 2020, https://www.cnbc.com/2020/06/04/cramer-the-pandemic-led-to-a-great-wealth-transfer.html (accessed April 30, 2021)

31 Joel Kotkin, "How America Is Reverting Back To The Feudal Age," *New York Post*, December 25, 2019, https://nypost.com/2019/12/25/how-america-is-reverting-back-to-the-feudal-age/ (accessed April 30, 2021)

32 Tom Donelson, *The Rise of National Populism and Democratic Socialism* (New York: Post Hill Press, 2017)

33 Tom Donelson, *The Rise of National Populism and Democratic Socialism* (New York: Post Hill Press, 2017)

34 Dr. Jonathan Geach, "Moving The Goalposts: Four Reasons It Is Safe To Open America," Medium, April 16, 2020, https://medium.com/@jbgeach/changing-the-goalposts-four-more-reasons-it-is-safe-to-open-america-560cfc0ab4c3 (accessed August 7, 2021)

35   Tom Donelson, Clara Del Villar, and JD Johannes, *Taxes and Social Security: The New Paradigm* (Marion, Iowa: Americas Majority Foundation, 2019),

36   Tom Donelson, Clara Del Villar, and JD Johannes, Taxes *and Social Security: The New Paradigm* (Marion, Iowa: Americas Majority Foundation, 2019), 5.

37   Matthew D. Dickerson and Frederico Bartels. "Republican Study Committee Budget Would Reclaim America's Future," Heritage Foundation, May 19, 2021, https://www.heritage.org/budget-and-spending/commentary/republican-study-committee-budget-would-reclaim-americas-fiscal (accessed August 7, 2021)

38   *Taxes and Social Security: The New Parad*igm (Americas Majority Foundation, 20XX)

39   *Taxes and Social Security: The New Paradigm* (Americas Majority Foundation, 20xx)

40   Matthew Dickerson and Frederico Bartels, "Republican Study Committee Budget Would Reclaim America's Fiscal Future," Daily Signal, May 19, 2021, https://www.dailysignal.com/2021/05/19/republican-study-committee-budget-would-reclaim-americas-fiscal-future/ (accessed May 29, 2021)

41   *Taxes and Social Security: The New Paradigm* (Americas Majority Foundation, 20xx)

42   Tom Donelson, *The Rise of National Populism and Democratic Socialism* (Post Hill Press, 2017)

43   We didn't ask our researchers whether the date the Social Security system would go bankrupt would be extended if these additional taxes were collected.

44   John Olson, "Payroll Taxes: The Good The Bad, and The Solution," Tax Foundation, August 2, 2016, https://taxfoundation.org/payroll-taxes-good-bad-and-solutions/ (accessed May 26. 2021)

45 Cllara Del Villar, Tom Donelson and JD Johannes, *Politics of Retirement: Report of Votres Over The Age of 50* (Marion Iowa: Americas Majority Foundation, 2019).

46 Tom Donelson, *From Trump To Le Pen: Where Populism Go* (Marion, Iowa: Americas Majority Foundation, 2017)

47 Tom Donelson, *The Rise of National Populism and Democratic Socialism: What Our Response Should Be (*New York: Post Hill Press, 2017), PAGE NUMBER TK

48 John McCormack, "Liz Cheney: 'We Cannot Become The Party of QAnon," National Review Online, February 6, 2021, https://www.nationalreview.com/corner/liz-cheney-we-cannot-become-the-party-of-qanon/ (accessed May 26, 2021)

49 Paul Mirengoff, "Liz Cheney Adopts GOP Talking Point," ON PAYROLL TAX RATES Power Line, February 4, 2021, CAN'T ACCESS THIS FOR TECHNICAL REASONS

50 Marco Respinti, "Marine Le Pen Succeeded By 'Breaking Into The Left," Acton Institute, April 24, 2017, https://www.acton.org/publications/transatlantic/2017/04/24/marine-le-pen-succeeded-breaching-left (accessed May 26, 2021)

51 "72 Percent See Trump As Model For Re[publican's Future," Rasmussen Reports, December 28, 2020, https://www.rasmussenreports.com/public_content/politics/general_politics/december_2020/72_of_republicans_see_trump_as_model_for_party_s_future (accessed August 7, 2021)

52 Clara Del Villar, Tom Donelson and JD Johannes, , *Politics of Retirement: Report On Voters Over 50* (Marion, Iowa: Americas Majority Foundation, 20xx)

53 Tom Donelson and JD Johannes, *Nordic Capitalism, Venezuelan Socialism, and Voter Perceptions,* (Marion, Iowa: Americas Majority Foundation, 2019)

54 Tom Donelson, *Winning 2016 and Moving Forward* (Marion, Iowa: Americas Majority Foundation, 2016). Tom Donelson and

JD Johannes, *Lessons for 2020* (Marion, Iowa: Americas Majority Foundation, 2018)

55   Amy Wax and Larry Alexander, "Paying The Price For The Breakdown of the Country's Bourgeois Culture," *Philadelphia Inquirer*, August 9, 2017, https://www.inquirer.com/philly/opinion/commentary/paying-the-price-for-breakdown-of-the-countrys-bourgeois-culture-20170809.html (accessed June 1, 2021)

56   Peter S. Goodman, "The Changing Face of Sweden: Boon or Burden?" *New York Times*, July 14, 2019.

57   David Montgomery, "AOC's Chief of Change," *Washington Post Magazine*, July 10, 2019, https://www.washingtonpost.com/news/magazine/wp/2019/07/10/feature/how-saikat-chakrabarti-became-aocs-chief-of-change/ (Accessed June 1, 2021)

58   Michael Cembalest, "Lost In Space: The Search For Democratic Socialism In The Real World," JP Morgan, June 24, 2019, https://privatebank.jpmorgan.com/content/dam/jpm-wm-aem/global/pb/en/insights/eye-on-the-market/lost-in-space-the-search-for-democratic-socialism-in-the-real-world-and-how-i-ended-up-halfway-around-the-globe-from-where-i-began.pdfl (accessed June 1, 2021)

59   Michael Cembalest, "Lost In Space: The Search for Democratic Socialism In The Real World," JP Morgan, June 24, 2019, https://privatebank.jpmorgan.com/content/dam/jpm-wm-aem/global/pb/en/insights/eye-on-the-market/lost-in-space-the-search-for-democratic-socialism-in-the-real-world-and-how-i-ended-up-halfway-around-the-globe-from-where-i-began.pdf (accessed June 1, 2021)

60   Michael Cembalest, "Lost In Space: The Search for Democratic Socialism In The Real World," JP Morgan, June 24, 2019, https://privatebank.jpmorgan.com/content/dam/jpm-wm-aem/global/pb/en/insights/eye-on-the-market/lost-in-space-the-search-for-democratic-socialism-in-the-real-world-and-how-i-ended-up-halfway-around-the-globe-from-where-i-began.pdf (accessed June 1, 2021)

61 David Sirota, "Hugo Chavez's Economic Miracle," *Salon*, March 6, 2013, https://www.salon.com/2013/03/06/hugo_chavezs_economic_miracle/ (accessed June 2, 2021)

62 Eric Liu and Nick Hanauer, "The True Origins of Prosperity," *Democracy*, Summer 2013, https://democracyjournal.org/magazine/29/the-true-origins-of-prosperity/ (accessed May 29, 2021)

63 Eric Liu and Nick Hanauer, "The True Origins of Prosperity," *Democracy*, Summer 2013, https://democracyjournal.org/magazine/29/the-true-origins-of-prosperity/ (accessed May 29, 2021)

64 John Harwood, "10 Questions With Bernie Sanders," CNBC, May 26, 2015, https://www.cnbc.com/2015/05/26/10-questions-with-bernie-sanders.html (accessed June 2, 2021)

65 Francesco Bianchi, Giada Bianchi, and Dongho Song, *The Long-Term Impact of The Covid-19 Unemployment Shock on Life Expectancy and Mortality Rates*, National Bureau of Economic Research Working Paper 23804, January 2021, https://www.nber.org/system/files/working_papers/w28304/w28304.pdf (accessed June 2, 2021)

66 Len Cabrera, "Mistake or Manipulation?" Alachua Chronicle, September 9, 2020, https://alachuachronicle.com/mistake-or-manipulation/ (accessed June 2, 2021)

67 Len Cabrera, "Mistake or Manipulation?" Alachua Chronicle, September 9, 2020, https://alachuachronicle.com/mistake-or-manipulation/ (accessed June 2, 2021)

68 Sharon Begley, "Influential Covid-19 Model Uses Flawed Method And Shouldn't Guide U.S. Policies, Critics Say," Stat, April 17, 2020, https://www.statnews.com/2020/04/17/influential-covid-19-model-uses-flawed-methods-shouldnt-guide-policies-critics-say/ (accessed May 29, 2021) THIS WAS EMBEDDED IN YOUR TEXT

69 "As U.S. Death Toll Surpasses 4,600, Fauci Says The Real Turning Point In Coronavirus Mitigation Won't Happen Until There's A Vaccine," *Washington Post*, April 1, 2020 https://www.

washingtonpost.com/world/2020/04/01/coronavirus-latest-news/ (accessed May 31, 2020)

70 Dr. Jay Bhattacharya, "A Sensible and Compassionate COVID-19 Strategy," American Institute for Economic Research, October 9, 2020 https://www.aier.org/article/a-sensible-and-compassionate-anti-covid-strategy/ (accessed June 2, 2021)

71 Dr. Jay Bhattacharya, " A Sensible and Compassionate COVID-19 Strategy," American Institute for Economic Research, October 9, 2020, https://www.aier.org/article/a-sensible-and-compassionate-anti-covid-strategy/ (accessed June 2, 2021)

72 Dr. Jay Bhattacharya, "A Sensible and Compassionate COVID-19 Strategy," American Institute for Economic Research, October 9, 2020, https://www.aier.org/article/a-sensible-and-compassionate-anti-covid-strategy/ (accessed June 2, 2021)

73 Yelp Local Economic Impact Report, September 2020, https://www.yelpeconomicaverage.com/business-closures-update-sep-2020.html (accessed June 2, 2020)

74 Jordan Schachtel, "How The White House Task Force Sank The Trump Presidency," American Institute of Economic Research, January 8, 2021, https://www.aier.org/article/how-the-white-house-covid-task-force-sank-the-trump-presidency/ (accessed June 3, 2021)

75 Jordan Schachtel, "How The White House COVID Task Force Sank The Trump Presidency," American Institute of Economic Research, January 8, 2021, https://www.aier.org/article/how-the-white-house-covid-task-force-sank-the-trump-presidency/ (accessed June 3, 2021)

76 Dr. Vinay Prasad, "Why Did Fauci Move The Herd Immunity Goal Posts?" Med Page Today, December 29, 2020, https://www.medpagetoday.com/opinion/vinay-prasad/90445 (accessed June 3, 2021)

77 Dr. Vinay Prasad, "Why Did Fauci Move The Herd Immunity Goal Posts?" Med Page Today, December 29, 2020, https://www.medpagetoday.com/opinion/vinay-prasad/90445 (accessed June 3, 2021)

78   Dr. Vinay Prasad, "Why Did Fauci Move The Herd Immunity Goal Posts?" Med Page Today, December 29, 2020, https://www.medpagetoday.com/opinion/vinay-prasad/90445 (accessed June 3, 2021)

79   Dr, Scott W. Atlas, "A Pandemic of Misinformation, " *Wall Street Journal,* December 22, 2020.

80   Dr. Scott W. Atlas, "A Pandemic of Misinformation," *Wall Street Journal,* December 22, 2020.

81   John Hinderaker, "The Obama Administration's Idea of a Crime..." Power Line, March 5, 2016, https://www.powerlineblog.com/archives/2016/03/the-obama-administrations-idea-of-a-crime.php (accessed June 3, 2021)

82   John Hinderaker, "The Obama Administration's Idea of a Crime..." Power Line, March 5, 2016, https://www.powerlineblog.com/archives/2016/03/the-obama-administrations-idea-of-a-crime.php (accessed June 3, 2021)

83   Dr. Pierre L. Gosselin, "NASA Vegetation Index: Globe combines Rapid Cooling Trend, Sahara Alone Shrinks 700,000 SqKm!" No Tricks Zone, February 24, 2021, https://notrickszone.com/2021/02/24/nasa-vegetation-index-globe-continues-rapid-greening-trend-sahara-alone-shrinks-700000-sq-km/?utm_source=rss&utm_medium=rss&utm_campaign=nasa-vegetation-index-globe-continues-rapid-greening-trend-sahara-alone-shrinks-700000-sq-km (accessed June 3, 2021)

84   Glenn Kessler, "Kerry's Flawed Claim That: "We Have Nine Years Left" To Avert The Climate Crisis," *Washington Post*, February 28, 2021, https://www.washingtonpost.com/politics/2021/02/22/kerrys-claim-that-we-have-nine-years-left-avert-climate-crisis/ (accessed June 1, 2021)

85   Jeff Tollefson, "Global Warming 'Hiatus' Debate Flares Up Again," *Nature*, February 24, 2016, https://www.nature.com/articles/nature.2016.19414 (accessed June 3. 2021)

86   Hinderaker footnote TK

87 For text of the bill, see https://leginfo.legislature.ca.gov/faces/bill-NavClient.xhtml?bill_id=201520160SB1161 (accessed June 3, 2021)

88 James Varney, "Skeptical Climate Scientists Coming In From The Cold," Real Clear Investigations, December 31, 2016, https://www.realclearinvestigations.com/articles/2016/12/31/skeptical_climate_scientists_coming_in_from_the_cold.html (accessed June 3, 2021)

89 Kevin Mooney, "House Probe Reveals Audit Detailing Climate Change Researcher's 'Double-Dipping,' *Daily Signal*, March 3, 2016, https://www.dailysignal.com/2016/03/02/house-probe-reveals-audit-detailing-climate-change-researchers-double-dipping-with-taxpayer-funds/ (accessed May 31, 2021) WIKIPEDIA SAYS THE AUDIT WAS CLOSED AND NO ACTION WAS TAKEN BUT I CAN FIND NO CONFIRMATION OF THIS

90 Robert Bradley, Jr., "Global Warming Scare Tactics Are No Substitute For Facts," Shale Directories, https://www.shaledirectories.com/blog-1/global-warming-scare-tactics-are-no-substitute-for-facts/?utm_source=rss&utm_medium=rss&utm_campaign=-global-warming-scare-tactics-are-no-substitute-for-facts (accessed June 3, 2021)

91 Robert Bradley, Jr., "Global Warming Scare Tactics Are No Substitute For Facts," Shale Directories, https://www.shaledirectories.com/blog-1/global-warming-scare-tactics-are-no-substitute-for-facts/?utm_source=rss&utm_medium=rss&utm_campaign=-global-warming-scare-tactics-are-no-substitute-for-facts (accessed June 3, 2021)

92 David M. Simon, "Paul Krugman Is A Global Warming Alarmist. Don't Be Like Him," Real clear Markets, January 16, 2020, https://www.realclearmarkets.com/articles/2020/01/16/paul_krugman_is_a_global_warming_alarmist_dont_be_like_him_104041.html (accessed June 3, 2021)

93 Joan Hoff Wilson, *Herbert Hoover: Forgotten Progressive* (Boston: Little, Brown, 1975), 68.

94   Steven Horwitz, "Herbert Hoover: Father of the New Deal," Cato Institute, 2011, https://www.cato.org/sites/cato.org/files/pubs/pdf/bp122.pdf (accessed June 3, 2021)

95   Jim Meyers, "15 Things Trump and Reagan Have In Common," Newsmax, August 3, 2015, https://www.newsmax.com/TheWire/trump-reagan-common-things/2015/08/03/id/665217/ (accessed June 1, 2021) THIS WAS EMBEDDED IN TEXT

96   Michael Lind, "The COVID Class War Heats Up," *Tablet*, March 16, 2021, https://www.ta,letmag.com/sections/news/articles/the-covid-class-war-heats-up-michael-lind (accessed June 10, 2021)

97   Tom Donelson, *Republicans Don't Have A Woman Gap, It is A Minority Gap* (Marion, Iowa: Americas Majority Foundation, 2014)

98   Robert Rector, "Marriage: America's Greatest Weapon Against Child Poverty," Heritage Foundation, September 10, 2010, https://www.heritage.org/poverty-and-inequality/report/marriage-americas-greatest-weapon-against-child-poverty-0 (accessed June 10, 2021)

99   Robert Rector, "Married Fathers: America's Greatest Weapon Against Child Poverty," Heritage Foundation, June 16, 2010, https://www.heritage.org/welfare/report/married-fathers-americas-greatest-weapon-against-child-poverty (accessed June 10, 2021)

100 Kay S. Hymowitz, "American Caste," *City Journal*, Spring 2012, https://www.city-journal.org/html/american-caste-13467.html (accessed June 10, 2021)

101 Sean Trende, *The Lost Majority: Why The future of Government Is Up for Grabs—And Who Will Take It* (New York: Palgrave Macmillan, 2012), 163.

102 Sean Trende, *The Lost Majority: Why The future of Government Is Up for Grabs—And Who Will Take It,* 163.

103 *Eric O'Keefe and Wisconsin Club for Growth vs. Francis Schmitz, John Chisholm, Bruce Landgraf, David Robles, Dean Nickel, and Gregory Peterson,* decided in the Eastern District of Wisconsin,

May 6, 2014, Case 14-c-139, https://www.wied.uscourts.gov/sites/wied/files/documents/opinions/Eric%20OKeefe.pdf (accessed June 10, 2021)

104 Victoria Taft, "Andy Ngo Unmasks Antifa In New Book And Warns, 'Antifa Lives and Thrives Only If America Dies,'"PJ Media, February 2, 2021, https://pjmedia.com/news-and-politics/victoria-taft/2021/02/02/andy-ngo-unmasks-antifa-in-new-book-and-warns-antifa-lives-and-thrives-only-if-america-dies-n1422325 (accessed August 8, 2021)

105 Victoria Taft, "Andy Ngo Unmasks Antifa IIn New Book And Warns, 'Antifa Lives And Thrives Only If America Dies,'" PJ Media, February 2, 2021, https://pjmedia.com/news-and-politics/victoria-taft/2021/02/02/andy-ngo-unmasks-antifa-in-new-book-and-warns-antifa-lives-and-thrives-only-if-america-dies-n1422325 (accessed August 8, 2021)

106 Natalie Escobar, "One Author's Controversial View: "In Defense of Looting,' NPR, August 27, 2020, https://www.npr.org/sections/codeswitch/2020/08/27/906642178/one-authors-argument-in-defense-of-looting (accessed June 10, 2021)

107 Brad Polumbo, "New Reporting Shows Kenosha Riots Hit Minority Communities Hardest," foundation for Economic Education, September 10, 2020, https://fee.org/articles/new-reporting-shows-kenosha-riots-hit-minority-communities-hardest/ accessed June 10, 2021)

108 "Fact Check: Kamala Harris Said She Supports 'Protests,' Not Riots," Reuters, October 29, 2020, https://www.reuters.com/article/uk-factcheck-kamala-harris-late-show-rio/fact-check-kamala-harris-said-she-supports-protests-not-riots-in-late-show-clip-idUSKBN27E34P (accessed June 10, 2021)

109 Isaac Schorr, "A Misleading Attempt To Bolster The "Mostly Peaceful' Riots Narrative," *National Review Online*, September 8, 2020, https://www.nationalreview.com/2020/09/a-misleading-attempt-to-bolster-the-mostly-peaceful-riots-narrative/ (accessed

August 8, 2021), This study combined peaceful protest with violent activity to make their case that protests were mostly peaceful. The violent activities were by their own admission mostly associated with Black Lives Matter.

110 While many neo-Nazi supported Trump in 2016, many of these same neo-Nazis supported Biden in 2020. Alt-right leader Richard Spencer, for example, switched from endorsing Trump in 2016 to endorsing Biden in 2020. This should not have been surprising, since alt-right views are in many ways mirrors of Antifa and the political left.

111 Everton Bailey, Jr., "Portland Mayor Says He'll Move After Protest Outside His condo Building Draws Arrests, Widespread Calls for Change," Portland *Oregonian*, September1, 2020, https://www.oregonlive.com/portland/2020/09/portland-mayor-says-hell-move-after-protest-outside-his-condo-building-draws-arrests-widespread-calls-for-change.html (accessed June 10, 2021)

112 Eoin Lenihan, "It's Not Your Imagination: The Journalists Writing About Antifa Are Often Their Cheerleaders," Quillette, May29, 2019, https://quillette.com/2019/05/29/its-not-your-imagination-the-journalists-writing-about-antifa-are-often-their-cheerleaders/ (accessed June 10, 2021)

113 Eoin Lenihan, "It's Not Your Imagination: The Journalists Writing About Antifa Are Often Their Cheerleaders," Quillette, May 29, 2019, https://quillette.com/2019/05/29/its-not-your-imagination-the-journalists-writing-about-antifa-are-often-their-cheerleaders/ (accessed June 10, 2021). Jason Wilson, "Occupy Ice: Activists Blockade Portland Building Over family Separations," *The Guardian*, June 20, 2018, https://www.theguardian.com/us-news/2018/jun/20/occupy-ice-portland-protest-immigration-family-separations (accessed June 10, 2021)

114 Eoin Lenihan, "It's Not Your Imagination: The Journalists Writing About Antifa Are Often Their Cheerleaders,' Quillette, May 29, 2019, ttps://quillette.com/2019/05/29/its-not-your-imagination-the-journalists-writing-about-antifa-are-often-their-cheerleaders/

Christopher Mathias, "Exposed: Military Investigating 4 More Servicemen for Ties To White Nationalist Group," Huffpost, April 27, 2019, https://www.huffingtonpost.ca/entry/white-national-ists-military-identity-evropa_n_5cc1a87ee4b0764d31dd839c (accessed June 10, 2021)

115 *Christiana Tah and Randolph McClain v, Global Witness Publishing and Global Witness,* decided by the U.S. District Court for the District of Columbia, Case 19-5132, decided March 19, 2021, https://www.cadc.uscourts.gov/internet/opinions.nsf/C5F7840A6FFFCF648525869D004ECAC5/$file/19-7132-1890626.pdf (accessed June 11, 2021). Judge Silberman's dissent begins on page 19.

116 *Christiana Tai and Randolph McClain v. Global Witness Publishing and Global Witness,* decided by the U.S. District Court for the District of Columbia, Case 19-5132, decided March 19, 2021, https://www.cadc.uscourts.gov/internet/opinions.nsf/C5F7840A6FFFCF648525869D004ECAC5/$file/19-7132-1890626.pdf (accessed June 11, 2021).

117 Tim Groseclose, *Left Turn: How Liberal Media Bias Affects The American Mind* (New York: St. Martin's Press, 2011), 215-16.

118 Tim Groseclose, *Left Turn: How Liberal Media Bias Affects The American Mind* (New York: St. Martin's Press, 2011) , 204,

119 Tim Groseclose, *Left Turn: How Liberal Media Bias Affects The American Mind* (New York: St. Martin's Press, 2011), 173.

120 Alexander Watson, "Poll Shows Media Censorship Cheated Voters of Second Term," CNS News, November 24, 2020, https://www.cnsnews.com/article/national/alexander-watson/poll-shows-me-dia-censorship-cheated-voters-vital-info-robbed (accessed June 11, 2021)

121 Stephen Green, "NYT Bombshell Essentially Boils Down To This: Trump Paid Millions in Taxes, Owes No Debt to Russia," PJ Media, September 28, 2020, https://pjmedia.com/vodkapundit/2020/09/28/

nyt-bombshell-trump-paid-millions-in-taxes-owes-no-debt-to-russia-wait-what-n974892 (accessed August 8, 2021)

122 Emma Cotton, "CNN's Brian Stelter Advocates Limiting A 'Liar's Reach,' Says It Isn't The Same As Censorship," *Washington Examiner*, January 31, 2021, https://www.washingtonexaminer.com/news/brian-stelter-cennsorship-harm-reduction (accessed June 11, 2021)

123 Emily Jashinsky, "Brian Stelter's Creepy Request of Big Tech Should Have Journalists Denouncing Him," *The Federalist*, February 3, 2021, https://thefederalist.com/2021/02/03/brian-stelters-creepy-request-of-big-tech-should-have-corporate-journalists-denouncing-him/ (accessed June 11, 2021)

124 Mark P. Mills, "Gat Government Out Of The Way of America's Oil, Gas Boom," Gannett op-ed appearing in Idaho *Statesman-Journal*, April 2, 2014, https://www.statesmanjournal.com/story/opinion/2014/04/11/get-government-out-of-the-way-of-americas-gas-oil-boom/7368123/ (accessed June 11, 2021)

30 Mark P. Mills, "Get Government Out Of The Way o America's Oil, Gas Boom," Gannett op-ed appearing in Idaho *Statesman-Journal*, April 2, 2014, https://www.statesmanjournal.com/story/opinion/2014/04/11/get-government-out-of-the-way-of-americas-gas-oil-boom/7368123/ (accessed June 11, 2021)

125

126 Nicholas Eberstadt. Derek Scissors, and Evan Abramsky, "America Is Petroleum-Independent, For Now," *National Review*, April 5, 2021, https://www.nationalreview.com/magazine/2021/04/05/america-is-petroleum-independent-for-now/ (accessed June 11, 2021)`

127 Michael Barone, "What's Trump Up To On Foreign Policy?" *Washington Examiner*, December 15, 2016, https://www.aei.org/articles/whats-trump-up-to-on-foreign-policy/ accessed June 18, 2021)

128 Michael Barone, "What's Trump Up To On Foreign Policy?" *Washington Examiner*, December 15, 2016, https://www.aei.org/